THE JEWISH QUARTERLY

The Jewish Quarterly is published four times a year
by The Jewish Quarterly Pty Ltd

Publisher: Morry Schwartz

ISBN 9781760645236 E-ISBN 9781743823392
ISSN 0449010X E-ISSN 23262516

ALL RIGHTS RESERVED.
No part of this publication may be reproduced, stored in a retrieval system
or transmitted in any form by any means electronic, mechanical, photocopying,
recording or otherwise without the prior consent of the publishers.

Essay © retained by the author

Subscribe online at jewishquarterly.com or email subscribe@jewishquarterly.com
Correspondence should be addressed to: The Editor, The Jewish Quarterly,
22–24 Northumberland Street, Collingwood VIC 3066 Australia
Phone +61 3 9486 0288 Email enquiries@jewishquarterly.com

The Jewish Quarterly is published under licence from the
Jewish Literary Trust Limited, which exercises a governance function.

UK Company Number: 01189861. UK Charity Commission Number: 268589.

Directors of the Jewish Literary Trust: Lance Blackstone (chair),
Devorah Baum, Ian Buruma, John Cohen, Shelly Freeman, Michael Mocatto,
Lorraine Solomon and Michael Strelitz.

Founding Editor: Jacob Sonntag.

Editor: Jonathan Pearlman. Associate Editors: Jo Rosenberg and Emma
Schwarcz. Assistant Publisher: Nomi Kaltmann. Management: Elisabeth
Young. Circulations: Ella Katz. Marketing and Partnerships: Gabriella Hills.
Design: John Warwicker and Tristan Main. Production: Marilyn de Castro.
Typesetting: Tristan Main.

Cover image by Bradley Cooper / Alamy Stock Photo

Issue 255, February 2024

THE JEWISH QUARTERLY

Dark Star

Elon Musk's dangerous turn

Richard Cooke is an award-winning foreign correspondent and author. His books include *Tired of Winning*, about Donald Trump's America, and a critical biography of the author Robyn Davidson. His next book is a cultural history of Wikipedia.

Editor's Note

This edition marks a new direction for The Jewish Quarterly.

The publication's aim – to feature the world's best writers and thinkers, exploring politics, history, culture and community – remains as urgent as ever. But the format is changing. Each issue will now feature one captivating long-form essay that deals with a pressing topic of the day. It's a unique format: it offers the depth of a book, but with the tightness and freshness of reportage.

Of course, the media has been moving in the opposite direction, towards ever shorter formats. Social media is now a major source of news and debate, and the result is often toxic, shallow and glib. In these online echo chambers, narrowness and hate – including antisemitism – are flourishing. It is a disturbing phenomenon that is now being overseen and encouraged by one of the world's richest, and arguably most innovative, people. In *Dark Star*, Richard Cooke examines Elon Musk and his transformation into an enabler of antisemitism. Musk is a fascinating figure: his sinister turn demands to be explored with the sort of depth and consideration that cannot be found in a Muskian tweet.

I appreciate that for some readers, this new format may seem daunting. I am confident, though, that any hesitation is about to disappear. Essays at this length are a craft: each will draw you in, hold you, and let you think.

Jonathan Pearlman

Dark Star
Elon Musk's dangerous turn

Richard Cooke

Nightfall

Elon Musk's interplanetary ambition is written onto the night sky. Amid the stars, visible to the naked eye, are the steady, blinking arcs of almost two thousand of his Starlink satellites, which together form what is called a "mega-constellation" of objects wreathing the Earth. While stargazers have compared their appearance to a train of light or a string of pearls, professional astronomers find them less beautiful. The view through high-powered telescopes is today "swarming with false stars", as one complaint put it, and this era of confusion is only beginning. Musk's company SpaceX has sought permission to launch as many as 42,000 satellites in all, and those who study light pollution suggest that one in ten "stars" visible to Americans and Europeans might soon be artificial.

Jonathan McDowell of the Center for Astrophysics, Harvard & Smithsonian, calls this change the "new space industrial revolution" and this is not an exaggeration. Of the 6905 satellites active in 2022, almost a third were added in a single year, and nearly all of them were launched by SpaceX. This tally does not include the less substantial objects that have taken flight over the same period. Musk's old car, for example, now cruises about 1.5 million kilometres away from its former owner, in orbit of the sun. It has a life-sized astronaut mannequin named Starman strapped into the driver's seat, a copy of Isaac Asimov's *Foundation* in the glovebox, and, if the battery still retains power, David Bowie playing on the stereo.

The new space industrial revolution is overwhelmingly the work of one man. There is space before Elon Musk, and space after Elon Musk. In 2018, his personal Tesla Roadster (with Starman at the wheel) was the test payload for the first Falcon Heavy rocket, one of several SpaceX launch vehicles that ended decades of aerospace inertia. Until then, both public and private actors had failed to match the ambition of the Space Race era, and it was just this malaise – punctuated by occasional, overpriced commercial satellite launches and the odd trip to the International Space Station – that Musk had vowed to change.

He knew little about rockets or astrophysics. Well-meaning experts preached caution or abandonment, and told him horror stories about the space follies of other rich men. One put together a compilation video of private rockets exploding, as a custom-made warning. Undeterred, Musk taught himself the physics of rocketry from vintage Russian textbooks, and, in 2002, cooked up a business plan that was, on paper, ridiculous. Rather than outsourcing, it called for building almost every piece of SpaceX's products in-house in Los Angeles, California. Reductions in manufacturing costs would come from using consumer electronics in place of the military-grade hardware favoured by Boeing and Lockheed Martin.

Boeing and Lockheed Martin would, in 2006, form a lucrative truce pact: the United Launch Alliance. Though its launches were expensive, ULA had a cosy relationship with NASA and the US Armed Forces, cemented by decades of generous lobbying. This meant that the US Air Force in particular disliked SpaceX, so much so that the fledgling company struggled to find an authorised launch site on the mainland United States. Instead, Musk was forced offshore, to a far-flung coral atoll called Omelek in the Marshall Islands. Omelek had little to recommend it except proximity to the equator (this offers a small shortcut to orbit), and sometimes, when resupply missions failed, SpaceX engineers would become stranded on the island without food.

At the same time, Musk had an even more implausible goal. Before he acquired the electric car company Tesla, the "newest" major player in the US car market was Chrysler, which had been established in 1925. With Tesla, his plan was to aggregate large numbers of lithium-ion batteries, the same type used in laptop computers, and place them in the chassis of carbon-fibre sports cars, which would then be sold direct to consumers over the internet. Tesla's cars would also be manufactured in Los Angeles, and the company soon found itself locked out of another closed shop. Other car makers turned out to have such a stranglehold over components that accessories as simple as sun visors were difficult to obtain (this is rumoured to be one reason early Teslas had no cup holders).

The scale of this dual ambition created almost inconceivable personal pressure

The adversaries in this two-front assault were formidable and well resourced. Alongside United Launch Alliance, Amazon's Jeff Bezos and Virgin's Richard Branson were also pouring millions into commercial space flight. The governments of Russia and China had interests to protect – previously, when Musk had travelled to Moscow to purchase decommissioned intercontinental ballistic missiles, he had been plied with vodka and then laughed out of the room. Moreover, General Motors, Ford, Nissan, Toyota and a small flotilla of Silicon Valley start-ups were unveiling their own electric cars. State-backed Chinese firms soon joined them.

The conditions of the wider economy were as unfavourable as they could be. Critical junctures in both Tesla and SpaceX – cash-intensive, loss-making businesses – coincided with the 2008 global financial crisis. Musk's personal fortune was already riding on these plays, and as venture capital began drying up, he begged Tesla's own executives to act as investors in their employer, like passengers bailing out a sinking ship. Friends urged him to kill either Tesla or SpaceX rather than allow both to die; instead, he was willing to flirt with total bankruptcy. He compared choosing between his companies to choosing between children, and took out loans with wealthy acquaintances to cover his household expenses.

In 2008, Tesla struggled to make payroll, and came within days of going under. The first three SpaceX launches failed. Only a small contract with the Malaysian government kept the firm from disaster. Musk micromanaged both enterprises throughout, sleeping under his desk or crashing on friends' couches. The scale of this dual ambition, and the circumstances of bringing it about, created almost inconceivable personal pressure. His weight ballooned and deflated. Deep shadows formed under his eyes. He began to have night terrors, thrashing and screaming out in pain while asleep. The British actor Talulah Riley, who became his second wife, watched his facial expression as more bad news poured in over email, and thought it was the prelude to a fatal heart attack.

Then it worked. All of it worked. Elon Musk revolutionised space flight and the car industry at the same time, and it made him the richest person in the world. When appraising him, this is a problem. His achievements are so stratospheric it is natural to try to diminish them. Naysayers pretend that these successes are down to luck, or unacknowledged government assistance, and in this view, the rise of Elon Musk is only a "zero interest rate phenomenon"; he is the winner of a liquidity lottery, a hype-man taking the credit from his anonymous engineers. It's not very convincing.

His unusual motives further complicate any assessment. Altogether, Musk heads six different companies: on top of his duties at Tesla and SpaceX, he runs The Boring Company, which aims to build better infrastructure by improving tunnelling technology; Neuralink, dedicated to experiments with brain implants; and xAI, an artificial intelligence company founded as a rival to OpenAI. Most controversially, he has also acquired the microblogging platform Twitter, since rebranded as X (for clarity, this essay uses the name Twitter), which he plans to turn into an "everything app", a bit like the Chinese all-in-one service WeChat. Each of these concerns, no matter how different from the others, falls under the same overarching mission: together they will help Musk save humanity.

SpaceX's satellite internet business, Starlink, already valued at US$30 billion, has the capacity to connect the entire world to high-speed broadband. Yet for Musk this was only an afterthought, a stepping stone. Starlink's real purpose, he has said, is to fund the construction of a city on Mars, just as the true purpose of Tesla is to end the era of fossil fuels. This ambition has been questioned and mocked. Sam Altman, CEO of OpenAI, has said that "Elon desperately wants the world to be saved. But only if he can be the one to save it". Nevertheless, this faith seems to be sincere.

He has maintained this commitment in private, and sometimes spent hours arguing with his partner that he should be allowed to die on Mars.

His very first contacts with the space industry, more than twenty years ago, were driven by visions of humanity's otherworldly future. Musk interrogated engineers about terraforming Mars with nuclear missiles, and asked how humans might one day live in glass biodomes. He wanted to send test batches of rodents to distant planets – they would need to reproduce en route, he was told, and these loads of "fucking mice" became a recurrent in-joke (they are the reason an early SpaceX flight carried a giant wheel of cheese). A millions-strong fanbase underwrites these ambitions with their devotion. When Musk was named *TIME* magazine's person of the year in 2021, a piece by three different writers said he "aspires to save our planet and get us a new one", and praised him as a "clown, genius, edgelord, visionary, industrialist, showman, cad".

Little more than two years later, this image is barely recognisable. The person of the year has since been called "the most dangerous antisemite in America". Ordinarily sober business publications report how Musk "regularly engages with antisemitic users" on a social media platform he owns. "Elon Musk insists he isn't an antisemite," the *Wall Street Journal* reported on 18 November 2023. "But this past week, the billionaire entrepreneur left many wondering." He had, that week, endorsed an antisemitic conspiracy theory suggesting Jews were responsible for fomenting racial hatred against whites. This was only the latest escalation in a feverish and sustained engagement with white nationalists.

One brake on more widespread condemnation of Musk's behaviour is shock verging on disbelief. What had happened to the self-described social liberal, who as late as September 2021 claimed that he "would prefer to stay out of politics"? His own politics, always indistinct (the *New York Times* called them "elusive", which in retrospect sounds like a euphemism) were now expressed as a string of social media "likes" and replies, hat-tips to some of the more notorious racist trolls in the world. Individually, these interactions could seem coincidental, even accidental, but as a pattern they are unmistakeable. Elon Musk was having open, cordial exchanges with Holocaust deniers, white nationalists and neo-Nazis. He knew who they were. He knew what it meant. So did they. Andrew Torba, CEO of the far-right social media platform Gab (who refuses to speak with non-Christian journalists, including Jews), was clear-eyed about what was happening.

> In under five years we went from having every single one of our guys banned from the big tech platforms to the richest man in the world noticing, naming, and waging total war on our largest enemy while running one of those platforms. Let that sink in. Keep the faith. We are winning.

Musk's Jekyll and Hyde transformation was so radical and repellent that some close associates wondered if he was on drugs. The same man who had once told President Donald Trump, to his face, that the so-called Muslim ban was wrong was now "liking" the anti-immigration online media posts of Paul Golding, a far-right British politician once jailed for anti-Muslim hate crimes. Inspired by one self-described "raging anti-semite", Musk had also set his fans against the Anti-Defamation League, a century-old anti-racism organisation dedicated to combating Jew hatred and other forms of discrimination. The ADL was forced to hire armed guards in the aftermath.

It was difficult to accept that Musk had developed these views, seemingly out of nowhere, and the form they took made it harder still. He was most at ease when expressing them from the gutter, slithering into the same digital ecosystem that sustains the lowest forms of online life, then feeding them with his patronage, subsidy and endorsement. Was he an out-and-out antisemite and racist? It was openly discussed – *The Atlantic* suggested he was an "inevitable" antisemite, who had started to blame Jews for his business failings. Yet the ADL itself, seldom reluctant in using that term, was careful never to apply it to Musk. Rather, the ADL tried to soothe him, even buying ads on his platform as a peace offering. Musk had a warm public discussion with Israeli prime minister Benjamin Netanyahu – and afterwards did it all again.

Placating Musk means avoiding the danger of direct confrontation, but it is also a symptom of bewilderment. The political turning of Elon Musk is so abrupt, so wild and unexpected, that it verges on the inexplicable, and speculations range from the psychological to the pharmaceutical. It might be rooted in childhood trauma. It might be a Kanye West–style public mental health episode. Perhaps Musk's politics haven't changed, but his interests have. Perhaps he is a lonely, angry white man who has wandered down a now-familiar pathway of online radicalisation, from which riches are no protection. Musk is a lifetime attention seeker who has said a lot of things that defy belief, and this is a dark version of the same. Maybe we are dealing with a personality that is simply self-destructive. There are clues and kernels of truth in these explanations, but also limitations. They fixate on one man. They treat Musk's views as an expression of his foibles and vices, proof of the cliché that great men have great flaws. They understand his hate foremost as a personal emotion closely held, an emotion which, like love, has its own indiscretions, flings and life-long relationships. Some see Musk's mind as a kind of fire that might be volatile and singe some fingers, but can nevertheless be contained, and used as a propellant to further the common good.

This misses the logic of Musk's actions, and what they mean. His chronically online nature means his beliefs are in flux, waxing and waning with surges of social media attention. This also means his personal relationships with Jews matter very little. The writer Elad Nehorai, who has kept a close eye on Musk's interactions and associations, told Israel's Ynetnews that "it's not really important whether Musk is truly antisemitic or not", and this is astute. Digital hatreds can be collective and impersonal, and in Musk's hands, they can also be commanded and controlled. A self-described "longtermist", he seems to understand online hate accounts through a prism of utility instead of morality. The style of this political signalling, which is sci-fi flavoured and full of memes and jokes, means it is taken less seriously than it ought to be. Though he is already preparing to send astronauts to the moon, Musk has been consistently underestimated, and now the danger he presents is being underestimated as well.

> *Musk has been consistently underestimated, and now the danger he presents is being underestimated as well*

The suite of his beliefs is also more complicated and subtle than it first appears. Making nice with trolls is conspicuous and draws attention, but just as important is a less visible affiliation with a cultural wave rippling through Silicon Valley. This nascent movement, sometimes called the "tech right", has seen other tech moguls turn towards the right side of politics as well, and has so many unusual and esoteric features that it has been described as "a religion in which the adherents are also the gods". It has little interest in traditional conservative American battlegrounds such as abortion and gun rights. Rather, it opposes equality because it believes equality is inefficient. Musk is not the first member of this loose affiliation to make contact with the far right. While arguments among tech barons about artificial intelligence or the promise of immortality might seem obscure or ridiculous, they have high stakes. They are really debates about the shape of the future, which always seems outlandish before it arrives – and these barons may decide what shape that future takes. This elite subculture also exists very much in a time and a place – Silicon Valley, California. Which is where, in 2020, while subject to a series of Covid lockdowns, Elon Musk decided to, as he put it, "take the red pill".

From lockdown to meltdown

The most detailed and best-sourced explanation for Elon Musk's political turning comes from Walter Isaacson's mammoth biography, *Elon Musk*. Published in September 2023, it describes a sequence of events that seem to have altered him: the drastic anti-Covid measures put in place by California Democrats, snubs by Democratic politicians, and Musk's estrangement from one of his children, Vivian Jenna Wilson, who is a trans woman. At age eighteen, she changed her gender identity and her name, vowing to have nothing to do with her father. "When Musk found out … he was generally sanguine," Isaacson writes. "But then Jenna became a fervent Marxist and broke off all relations with him. 'She went beyond socialism to being a full communist and thinking that anyone rich is evil,' he said." Musk blamed her progressive Santa Monica school.

In 2020, California's response to Covid-19 shuttered Tesla factories at a crucial moment (though in Muskworld, all moments in the run-up to Mars are crucial). He was willing to break the law to prevent production delays, and though he extracted enough concessions to keep assembly lines flowing, his sense of alienation from the left remained. By mid-year his tweets were exhibiting a new vehemence towards marginalised groups.

In July he turned his ire on the pronouns used by trans and non-binary people, tweeting that "Pronouns suck", until he was called out by his then-partner, the singer and artist Grimes. "I love you but please turn off ur phone or give me a dall [*sic*]", she tweeted at him, "I cannot support hate. Please stop this. I know this isn't your heart." While she later deleted her response, his tweet remained. He began sending her memes and tweets that were so reactionary she wondered if they came from 4chan, a notorious internet message board and far-right breeding ground. Democratic politicians seem to have played a part in this rift too. When the Biden White House commended auto executives for their progress on electric cars, it had a habit of neglecting Tesla, praising companies with unionised workforces instead. Democrats criticised the amount of tax paid as well, though Musk was then probably the largest individual taxpayer in US history.

Elon Musk identifies another, less-emphasised, catalyst: in 2022, it was revealed that Musk had been accused of sexual harassment by a former flight attendant, when *Business Insider* alleged he offered her a horse in exchange for an erotic massage. Musk blamed a liberal one-time friend for leaking the story, and tried to paint the revelations as a political witch hunt. Soon after, he renounced his long-standing ballot box support for the Democratic Party. After claiming he had never before voted Republican, Musk backed

Republican candidates in the 2022 US midterm elections, and went on to launch the presidential campaign of Florida governor Ron DeSantis on Twitter itself. (Coinciding with a teething period for the site, their video interview was beset by technical glitches.)

Father figures

Isaacson's biography anchors Musk's transformation in psychological traits originating in his brutal childhood. An exhausting figure emerges: lonely and emotionally stunted, he lives in a cacophony of stress, most of it self-inflicted, much of it avoidable. His immediate family and former partners talk about his "drama magnetism", his fearlessness and his fervour. He has a weakness for draining and combative personal relationships. He enters eerie, blank-faced trance states, in which his already limited ability to read others' emotions shuts down altogether. These patterns grind on Musk himself as well as on the people around him, until their repetition feels not only monotonous, but fateful. Autism, PTSD and bipolar disorder are all offered as possible diagnoses. Sociopathy, which also maps, is not.

Musk's achievements seem to bring him fleeting relief instead of joy. His mission to preserve the flame of human consciousness is distinct from warm feelings towards fellow humans. It becomes, more often, a licence for casual sadism. When he screams at junior employees and fires them, the rationale is always at hand: they are letting down the team, and if the team fails, humankind is in trouble. This principle is applied up the chain as well. When Musk decides Google co-founder Larry Page is too cavalier about the existential risk from artificial intelligence, he poaches top engineers from Google's AI programme, and criticises Page in harsh enough terms that their relationship breaks down. Musk also allegedly had an affair with the wife of Google's other co-founder, Sergey Brin, which caused Brin to divest his Tesla shares and file for divorce. Both Page and Brin had been crucial investors in Tesla when it needed a lifeline.

For Isaacson, this pattern of wounding and retaliation, made congruent by an urgent sense of mission, all stems from Musk's relationship with his father. Errol Musk is a Rosetta stone that deciphers everything, an outsized character who fathered two children with a stepdaughter half his age, once shot dead two home intruders, and refuses still to say that he is proud of Elon. His shadow is immense, and those closest to Elon Musk notice that, at his most cruel, he uses phrases his father once did. In his interviews with Isaacson, the elderly Errol Musk comes across as more and more unhinged, until he is a fully-fledged Covid and election truther. Isaacson notes a similar conspiratorial tendency in Elon, "which made him believe that much of his negative press was due to the hidden agendas or corrupt interests of the people who own the news organizations". A less Freudian explanation was that father and son were culturally similar, wealthy men being influenced by the same right-wing material online. Elon at one stage tweeted that his pronouns were "Prosecute/Fauci", a barb aimed at President Biden's chief medical adviser. (In response, Elon's brother Kimbal told him he was being a "fucking idiot".)

> **Musk is hardly the only tech leader who grew up a bullied nerd**

But Isaacson applies this emotional archaeology to everything, even to Musk's purchase of Twitter. "Twitter was the ultimate playground," he writes, in one of the book's less persuasive passages:

As a kid, he was beaten and bullied on the playground, never having been endowed with the emotional dexterity needed to thrive on that rugged terrain. It instilled a deep pain and sometimes caused him to react to slights far too emotionally, but it also is what girded him to be able to face the world and fight every battle fiercely. When he felt dinged up, cornered, bullied, either online or in person, it took him back to a place that was super painful, where he was dissed by his father and bullied by his classmates. But now he could own the playground.

This tendentious idea stops short of the obvious conclusion: that the bullied had become the bully. But Musk is hardly the only tech leader who grew up a bullied nerd. When Musk began acquiring Twitter, the *New York Times* found an even less likely root cause from childhood. Musk's stated reasons for leaving South Africa as a young adult included avoiding compulsory military service for the apartheid regime, which he called "fascist". "It is unclear what role his childhood – coming up in a time and place in which there was hardly a free exchange of ideas and where government misinformation was used to demonise Black South Africans – may have played in that decision." This guesswork would come to feel further and further off the mark.

There is an alternative explanation for Musk's metamorphosis that avoids the dead ends of this armchair psychology. He is not the first tycoon who became pitiless at the top or on the way up, nor the first to feel underappreciated and set upon. Drifting to the right in middle age is a cliché, and many executives have enduring hate affairs with regulation. According to one theory, Musk's politics only *appear* to have changed. Underneath, for the decisions that really count, there is the constancy of serving his business interests.

Both the car company and the aerospace concern needed subsidy on the way up, and tax breaks, deregulation and union-busting once well established. The left's love of electric cars made for a marriage of convenience; once they were championing pandemic restrictions instead, the alliance was broken. There is no reason to expect political constancy in billionaires. It ignores their interests. Ten-digit fortunes are often tied to changes in government, especially in industries where government funds play an outsized role.

In this version, there is nothing mysterious about Musk's "apparent transformation from politically taciturn Obama donor to compulsive sharer of cringe-inducing conservative memes", as Eric Levitz put it in *New York Magazine*. "Musk is not only an identifiable political type but a familiar one," he wrote. "In many respects, he is a conservative in the mold of Donald Trump." Both were warm towards Democrats when Democratic industry policy suited them, and both became Republicans when these boosts were no longer as useful. Levitz speculates that a sense of personal grievance, fuelled by slights from Democratic politicians (Obama in Trump's case, Senator Elizabeth Warren in Musk's), completed the change.

Yet Musk's politics often stray from the path of pecuniary self-interest. His Twitter acquisition is estimated to have burned most of its US$44 billion valuation in less than a year, one of the most rapid destructions of value in media history. Though Musk is angered by the losses, and sometimes blames them on enemies, he is willing to endure them. On the popular Real Talk with Zuby podcast, Musk said that freedom of speech was "pretty expensive", and that so far his changes to Twitter moderation policies were costing the business about "$2 billion a year". If he is playing 4D chess, many of his moves are sacrifices with no material in return.

Another form of materialism may have driven him to the right: Social Darwinism. Just as Musk believes the laws of physics are the true bottom line in business, so his notion of social relations begins with biology. "Consciousness should be thought of as a tiny candle in a vast darkness that could easily go out," Musk has written. "We should do anything possible to keep that flame alive." This begins at home – he is a natalist concerned by low birth rates, and has fathered eleven known children with three different mothers. Grimes identified fertility concerns as being at the root of his transphobia: "It came down to pretty much every way that you transition can cause fertility issues," she told *WIRED* magazine. "I was like, OK, you don't hate trans people, you hate woke culture. I get that it can be annoying, and you have concerns about the fertility thing."

Musk's other beliefs are ideologically slippery, and at least once he has called himself a socialist (with conditions). Around 2020 he also seemed to become more ascetic, abandoning many possessions and choosing rather depressing living spaces (perhaps he listened to some of his daughter's critique of billionaires). He is a continuing, though less vocal, advocate of universal basic income, an issue that drove him to support the outsider presidential candidacy of Andrew Yang, a Democratic contender in 2020. There are the usual hypocrisies, too. He is a free speech absolutist who makes libel threats, a capitalist who praises communist China, a climate-change crusader who once used a private plane for the 56-kilometre trip between San Francisco and San Jose.

His politics are hard to pin down in practice as well as in theory. Is he an ideological tycoon, like the Koch brothers or George Soros, a font of dark money flowing to think tanks and candidates for office? Does he use his money tactically for his version of a greater good, like those in the effective altruism movement?

Is he an executive philosopher in the mould of Peter Thiel, who first hones his ideas and then tries to enact them through political kingmaking? Though he has been compared to Henry Ford and Howard Hughes, he may be closer to Rupert Murdoch: purchasing Twitter makes him the twenty-first-century equivalent of the newspaper proprietors and cable news mavens of the past, at a nexus of cultural, political and financial power. When the Murdochs fired the Fox News host Tucker Carlson, Musk's Twitter picked him up.

No politics is formed in isolation, and Musk's turning says as much about the shifting allegiances of Silicon Valley as it says about him. The historian Jill Lepore has termed "Muskism" a new form of hyper-capitalism, and traces its influences to early technocrats, twentieth-century science-fiction writing and the poisoned irony and antisocial edge of the present-day online milieu. Muskism is now firming into a new form of politics as well, whose consequences look to be more far-reaching and sinister.

> *He has been allowed a degree of control over space that was once unthinkable*

Musk is also filling a vacuum. He exists because of a failure of governments. His success was made possible by the decay of an older politics, a politics grown stale with public–private partnerships and cronyism. The cynicism of military-industrial lobbying and contracting, and the hollowing-out of state capacity and function, left space open for him. Every US president since Obama has been relieved to outsource space exploration to the private sector. Musk revitalised the aerospace industry, and in return, he has been allowed a degree of control over space that was once unthinkable for a private citizen, just as its true importance is becoming obvious.

This makes understanding Elon Musk's beliefs a pressing task, even an urgent one, as vital as diagnosing the ideological bent of a whole country. Underneath the dad jokes is a gravitational pull felt across business, politics and culture. If he is a genuine antisemite, then he combines that ancient hatred with an ominous reach that is entirely new. If he is not, then identifying why he makes common cause with antisemites is no less important. Musk's change of heart, his journey from a half-interested liberal to a revanchist right-winger and racist troll, is doubly attention-worthy because he is not alone. Despite a reputation for being politically homeless, he has affinities with a burgeoning and unusual political ideology rooted in the tech world, an odd strain of hierarchical futurism so fresh it has yet to settle on a name.

The stakes could hardly be higher. Already unmistakeable in energy politics and the culture war, his influence now extends to foreign policy and the conduct of modern warfare. The upper ranks of American diplomacy and military understood they had some reliance on Musk – since the Space Shuttle's decommissioning, US astronauts needed him to reach space, for example. It was only after the Russian invasion of Ukraine that they realised how beholden they were to one man.

The real front line

The Russia–Ukraine War is a throwback, a war of conquest in continental Europe, fought through incremental offensives and counteroffensives, stalemate and entrenchment. Even its mud is redolent of 1914, and this obscures one of its tactical realities: that it is also the first true internet war. Cyberattacks and patriotic bloggers played bit parts in the conflicts of the early twenty-first century, but only in this bitter confrontation has mobile broadband technology become central to shaping the battlefield.

Drones might be the most feared agent of that change. Not only the Turkish-made Bayraktar TB2 drones, which scored early successes for the Ukrainians (their black-and-white, high-aerial footage of Russian convoys being obliterated endured as images), but also shop-bought drones: the kind sold in toy stores, the same ones flown by farmers and amateur photographers. These are a crucial weapon of the Ukrainian counteroffensive. Readily available, cheap enough to buy in bulk and difficult to shoot down, they are capable of striking targets on land and sea, even behind enemy lines.

This last capability illuminates Elon Musk's walk-on role in the Russia–Ukraine War. He has a habit of inserting himself into major events to which he has little connection. When the world was transfixed by Thai schoolboys trapped in a flooded cave in 2018, he offered to design a submarine to rescue them. And when he was rebuffed by the cave diver heading the rescue operation, Musk called the man a paedophile, twice.

While he does have a charitable foundation, he prefers philanthropy from the hip: spontaneous, almost impulsive gifts of services or expertise, often brokered in public over social media. This publicity-rich method can be speedy and effective. When the state of South Australia suffered the risk of blackouts during its clean energy rollout, Tesla committed to building the world's largest battery there, and after a Twitter back-and-forth with Australian billionaire Mike Cannon-Brookes, Musk upped the ante: "Tesla will get the system installed and working 100 days from contract signature or it is free. That serious enough for you?" He made the deadline.

In the aftermath of the Russian march on Ukraine, Musk had another of these dramatic social media exchanges. This time the

Ukrainian vice prime minister Mykhailo Fedorov beseeched him directly: "@elonmusk while you try to colonize Mars – Russia try to occupy Ukraine! While your rockets successfully land from space – Russian rockets attack Ukrainian civil people! We ask you to provide Ukraine with Starlink stations and to address sane Russians to stand." Musk responded less than a day later with a tweet liked more than 760,000 times: "Starlink service is now active in Ukraine. More terminals en route." The service would also be free, Musk revealed in time. Starlink would become a vital electronic lifeline to the world, in lieu of Ukraine's shattered telecommunications infrastructure.

It was significant, and canny, that Fedorov made his appeal in public, but not everyone was impressed. "In that moment, Elon Musk, the man, seemed to be acting almost like a state of his own, a foreign entity that people around the world can call on for humanitarian aid the way they might call on a government," Marina Koren wrote in *The Atlantic*, before offering some comfort. Musk's "outsize reputation", she assured readers, "doesn't always match what he can actually control". Internally at SpaceX, the company's president, Gwynne Shotwell, argued that private subsidy of the Ukrainian war effort was a mistake. She was negotiating a US$145 million contract with the Pentagon, which would fund Starlink on behalf of the Ukrainians, and was exasperated when Musk decided to continue regardless: "The hell with it ..." he tweeted, "even though Starlink is still losing money & other companies are getting billions of taxpayer $, we'll just keep funding Ukraine govt for free." He got half a million likes. Shotwell thought he had "succumbed to the bullshit on Twitter".

It was also an opportunity for Musk to demonstrate what he could "actually control". The digital nature of the conflict meant Starlink determined the kinetic battlefield to an unprecedented degree. In October 2022, on the Crimean front, Kyiv's generals encountered Musk's wishes as an almost physical presence, a line of invisible fencing. As Ukrainian forces approached Russian-occupied areas, their internet terminals stopped working. At first soldiers thought it might be a technical glitch, interference from the pressures of combat. More senior leadership suspected that Musk was putting a curb on offensive actions with geofencing. They worried when he promoted a half-baked peace plan that involved territorial concessions to Russia. Almost a year later, Isaacson's book revealed what had really happened. In the waters around Sevastopol, Ukrainian forces had been conducting a submarine drone attack on Russian warships when the explosive-packed drones suddenly "lost connectivity and washed ashore harmlessly" before reaching their targets. Starlink had failed on the front lines once more, and not by accident. According to the book, Musk had ordered limitations to Starlink's range, to prevent these offensive incursions.

> *Whatever was happening on the ground, Musk controlled the upper limits of the sky above it*

Fedorov pleaded directly over Twitter once again: "I just want you – the person who is changing the world through technology – to know this," he said, begging Musk to switch the network back on. Musk refused. He had been speaking with Russian officials, who had warned him a direct attack on Crimea could trigger a nuclear response. "How am I in this war?" he said to Isaacson. "Starlink was not meant to be involved in wars. It was so people can watch Netflix and chill and get online for school and do good peaceful things, not drone strikes." He also clarified that he had not switched anything off – from the beginning of the conflict, Ukrainians' access to Starlink in contested territory had never been switched on.

Some called it treason. Musk was, they said, undermining the US State Department's policy on Ukraine. Others attacked the lack of wisdom that had granted him these powers in the first place. Other European militaries began an urgent search for a Starlink alternative so as not to find themselves in the same position. Musk said he had spoken with Putin personally, and then denied it. There were questions about the ethical contours of his intervention, as though it were all a vast, real-life trolley problem.

By October 2023, the Russians had withdrawn most of their Black Sea Fleet, because of constant harrying by Ukrainian drones and missiles, which had by then killed senior naval commanders, damaged vessels and made a major shipyard unusable. Could an earlier, Starlink-aided drone attack on the Black Sea Fleet have shortened the war? And why had the decision been in the hands of a lone individual who holds no public office? Several foreign policy observers thought Musk was repeating Putinist talking points. The Russians knew how to flatter credulous and well-positioned foreigners, while priming them with the Kremlin's preferred lines.

Musk's own admission – that Starlink had been geofenced for the whole war – had serious implications. It meant Musk could not only end the advance of a foreign military with a word, but also set the shape of that advance beforehand, making hard boundaries for the conflict, by himself and in secret. Few individuals have been so central to a war effort since the duelling atomic physicists of World War II. Whatever was happening on the ground, Musk controlled the upper limits of the sky above it.

Other countries recognised these ramifications, often too late. China realised Starlink could circumvent its "Great Firewall" internet censorship regime, and sought assurances that it would not be used for such a purpose (Musk agreed). Taiwan began work on a Starlink-like system of its own, in case of invasion. In the *New Yorker*, US officials complained about the "degree of dependency that the US now has on Musk in a variety of fields, from the future of energy and transportation to the exploration of space". They mentioned that Musk also controls the largest nationwide network of electric vehicle chargers in the United States, making him critical to the future rollout of EVs, whether they are Teslas or not. This matrix of power has been called a "shadow rule".

Though grave, the situation was also darkly comedic. The "guy who shouldn't be there" is a staple of military satire, and generals and heads of state had to watch helplessly as Musk posted his way through international relations. As well as having public conversations with senior politicians, he was throwing things open to civilians too. On 10 September 2022, just before the foiled Ukrainian attack, he tweeted, "I've been up all night trying to think of any possible way to de-escalate this war" and received this reply: "Might be a good idea to take Starlink offline for the terminals used on the frontlines. Could encourage them to reconsider their position on advancing towards Crimea and leading the world further into the brink of total war."

It was from a Twitter user named Ian Miles Cheong, an online political commentator with a substantial conservative fanbase, mostly in the United States. What makes him unusual is his origin story: Cheong, a former Reddit moderator who lives in Malaysia, has built his audience solely through posts that pander to American conservatives. Like many present-day figures on the post-cable television right, he cycled through several attention-seeking alter egos before settling on his final form.

He is as much a persona as a person, a new-media figure developed via experiments in virality. At last count he had 865,000 Twitter followers. That he appears to play a critical role in the Russia–Ukraine War must be a surprise even to him. He has real influence, only one step removed: Ukraine relies on Elon Musk, and Elon Musk listens to Ian Miles Cheong. The richest man in the world seeks his advice, then praises Cheong's counsel and acts on it. It is an outcome of almost exhilarating stupidity.

For centuries, diplomacy rested on carefully attuned language. Diplomats were expected to be shrewd and wise, schooled in history and languages. It goes almost without saying that a shit-posting social media account is the opposite of all this, almost a mockery of it. And yet thanks to Elon Musk, figures like Ian Miles Cheong have more purchase on international affairs than the editors of *Foreign Affairs*. What is apparently trivial or unserious is in fact deathly serious. Because of Starlink, a poster in a Kuala Lumpur bedroom is directly linked to the Ukrainian front lines.

The language of power still treats internet chatter as beneath consideration, unimportant almost by definition. Like the Ukrainians, we find ourselves suddenly surprised: it is social media, not cable or newspapers or conclaves, that now sits at the epicentre of power. Like it or not, the first internet troll tycoon defines an era as much as the first internet troll president of the United States.

Troll philanthropy

Is Elon Musk funny? This question might seem trivial or even distasteful in the context of talking about hate speech. Yet it is integral to his self-image. Musk seems to have a David Brent–like need to be admired as a comedic talent as well as a business leader.

And he can *seem* funny, when the occasion calls for it. His deadpan voice – clipped, still faintly South African – comes out the side of his mouth, as though he's a screwball-period comic chewing a cigar. He did a credible job hosting *Saturday Night Live*, where he joked that, despite his Asperger's, he could run "human in emulation mode". His affectless expression is arranged around a wry smile. He has an odd, stiff-necked posture, the result of an injury he sustained tackling a sumo wrestler to the ground at a party.

Pun-heavy gags are laced throughout his businesses. He has called himself the "Chief Twit" and "Treelon Musk", and the model names of Tesla's cars spell out "sexy" (S 3 X Y). For a time, some Tesla models could make simulated fart sounds until regulators intervened, and when they did Musk called them the "fun police". He requested a real hovercraft full of eels at his second wedding (like many nerds of his generation, Musk is a Monty Python fan) and his request was granted. This childishness, or childlike energy, if you prefer, extends to insults, defiance and provocation of regulators, and a prankish disdain for rules. When the Federal Aviation Administration told him not to launch a rocket, he did it anyway.

This mugging gets him into trouble. He smoked a joint while appearing on the Joe Rogan podcast (the BBC, with pleasing redundancy, described it as "containing a mix of tobacco and marijuana – dried leaves and flowering parts of the female cannabis plant"). Because SpaceX held federal contracts which mandate a drug-free workplace, twelve months of government-ordered drug tests followed, for Musk and his 6000 SpaceX staff. After tweeting that he would take Tesla private at $420 a share, a figure which most took as a drug reference (420 is a slang reference to cannabis), the Securities and Exchange Commission investigated him, and investors sued him. The final sum he paid for Twitter was $54.20 a share.

The antics can grate. Purchasing Twitter has enhanced Musk's ability to make a joke or meme go viral, something he seems to want very badly. He reportedly fired an engineer who told him why the @elonmusk account was getting fewer interactions. Prioritising paid-for blue-check accounts means the most prominent replies to his tweets tend to be from adoring fans. It means he can, for a moment, create the zeitgeist. The Australian comedian Illy Bocean summed it up this way:

> elon musk has all the money in the world and could be having every experience on this earth that is out of reach to the rest of us. but the one thing he wants is the thing he can't have: a world convinced that he's very funny and cool, and not a cringe middle-aged redditor.

Musk's standard comedic mode is trolling. He has been called "a troll who got lucky" (*The Independent*), a "try-hard" troll going after the Donald Trump template (*The Atlantic*), "the king of trolls in an age of troll politics" (*The Guardian*), and "an adept social-media troll" (Yahoo! Finance) who purchased Twitter mainly as an act of trolling. Musk is called a troll so often it's worth returning to the term's origin, which has nothing to do with cavern-dwelling creatures from Norse mythology. Rather, the word comes from the art of fishing, especially the practice of dragging a lure behind a moving boat. It is a method that involves repeat provocations, working the same areas at different depths or speeds. It requires deception. Bites come from inquisitiveness and anger as well as hunger. True online trolling is more than abuse, and involves shifting modes of entrapment to provoke a response.

An internet company – PayPal – made Musk's first fortune, and he understood how to manifest and control online attention very early on. He has been called the first internet celebrity, and his celebrity rose in tandem with social media (he now has the most followers of any account on Twitter). He was unusually open, not only about Tesla's aims but about some of its problems as well. He invited competition, going as far as offering patents to other car companies for free. His 2006 blog post titled "The Secret Tesla Motors Master Plan (just between you and me)" was irreverent about its supreme ambition: "to help expedite the move from a mine-and-burn hydrocarbon economy towards a solar electric economy". This style of communication, which was direct, personable and ironic, set the template for how other companies managed their online brand presence.

This exuberance can also conceal less-flattering realities. The *Washington Post* called this "the fundamental paradox of Musk",

> He has a feel for the spontaneity and the immediacy of roiling online conversation

that he is "both our Thomas Edison and that kid in school who made up fantastical stories about what he did on summer vacation". There are websites that track his broken promises, and even his supporters concede that he is prone to announce products before they're ready. As with Donald Trump, there is an ongoing discussion about whether or not Musk really believes what he says. They argue that these impossible deadlines serve an internal purpose, spurring on employees, and that he delivers – most of the time. Product announcements and publicity stunts are indistinguishable.

While this edgy online behaviour has won Musk many fans, it has also bred contempt. The PR executive turned tech commentator Ed Zitron thinks Musk is an avatar of nihilistic, socially corrupting late capitalism, the "rot king" or "Baloney King", "one of the world's most prolific liars" who is "constantly embellishing with the full knowledge that at his scale, people have to cover what he says, even if it's complete nonsense". Having learnt to manipulate legacy media by making grand announcements (which attract fanfare everyone is later too embarrassed or forgetful to retract), Musk upped the ante by drawing in social media and financial markets too.

Tesla has not released a car with a fully automated self-driving mode (though on his first date with Grimes, Musk did remove his hands from the steering wheel and close his eyes while they were on the freeway). The humanoid robots he promised are yet to arrive. When Musk challenged the founder of Facebook to a public cage fight and Mark Zuckerberg accepted (he is an accomplished amateur competitor in Brazilian jiu-jitsu), the details kept changing. Musk had spoken to the Italians, and the fight would take place in the Colosseum. Then it would be at Zuckerberg's house instead. Suddenly, Musk's bad back needed surgery. "We can all agree Elon isn't serious," Zuckerberg finally posted on his own microblogging site, Threads. It was time to move on.

It is the kind of publicity-rich trolling Musk excels at. He has a feel for the spontaneity and the immediacy of roiling online conversation, the quantum "just joking" state of meaning and not meaning something at the same time. He has even innovated in this area – during the defamation lawsuit brought by Vernon Unsworth, the cave diver he accused of paedophilia, Musk's lawyer tried a neologism of his own: the "pedo guy" insult was a "JDART", he suggested: a Joking, Deleted, Apologised For, Responsive Tweet. Taking the stand, Musk claimed that calling someone a paedophile was a non-specific insult from his rambunctious South African youth, not a specific allegation that Unsworth was a child molester. The jury believed him.

Another of Musk's lawyers said he was "just an impulsive kid with a terrible Twitter habit". It was an odd description of a man in his fifties, but for a time it obscured what he was doing. His tweeting was so prolific, and so ironic, that it seemed plausible he had affirmed the online statements of career antisemites by mistake. It was a kind of alibi. Musk's regular audience was used to not taking him too seriously. Yes, he seemed to be boosting discrimination, but he had also once boosted a joke cryptocurrency named Cum Rocket. It was distinct from a ringing endorsement. It took time for the incidences to accumulate into a pattern, and for the pattern to form a devolutionary trend.

The believer

One of the first profiles of Musk ever written, by the *Salon* journalist Mark Gimein in 1999, identified the young entrepreneur as a "believer". Gimein guessed rightly how crucial this quality would prove. "What his backers are looking for," he wrote, "is someone whose very ignorance of corporate manners allows him to induce a whole company to come together and embark on an ill-defined but promising course." An enhanced, all-encompassing version of this "ill-defined but promising course" now inspires millions of fellow believers, some to the point of sycophancy. Even Musk's ex-wives and his bruised former executives still talk about "the mission" unironically. The writer Edward Niedermeyer, in his critical account of Tesla, *Ludicrous*, likened Musk fans to cult members.

Though the adulation he receives is sometimes cult-like, Musk's position is more kingly than messianic. On Twitter he holds court. He laughs, and his people laugh too. There, he is petitioned by both commoners and people of rank, and can grant the wishes of each (the idea to blast his car into space, for example, came from a fan's request). The deference extends beyond fanboys: when Musk announced that Tesla would be leaving California, municipalities jockeyed for his attention through their official Twitter accounts. His subjects are protective of him – there is a sense of *lèse-majesté*: criticism or scepticism is treated not just as a personal insult, but as a threat to humanity's future. One "Musketeer", who produced an illustrated book of Musk's tweets, described herself as "enraged" by sceptical press about him: "What he's doing is dire and essential for human survival," she told The Verge. "This is my future, too. And this is my planet, too."

Why do the fans of the richest man in the world see him as vulnerable, or embattled? This apparent contradiction rests on a subtle interplay between Musk's public identity, Tesla as a brand and Tesla as a stock, all of which have spent periods under siege. Until recently, driving a Tesla was synonymous with being a card-carrying liberal, which meant facing real hostilities in the culture war. Tesla drivers were even targeted physically, by a red-state subculture named "rolling coal". Coal rollers are diesel trucks modified to spew acrid black smoke from their exhaust, which is then released over Teslas, Priuses and occasionally cyclists encountered on-road. The idea has been floated that Musk's political turn might be a cover, and that his new-found right-wing opinions and EV Cybertruck are only a means of softening conservative opposition to buying Teslas.

Tesla as a company was also targeted. Few other stocks have attracted so many attacks from short sellers. For years, there was little relationship between Tesla's balance sheets and its share price, and the vultures of the financial sector smelled sickness, flocking to the invalid and waiting for it to become a corpse. They sensed an inevitable correction, the moment Musk's fanboys abandoned him and his absurd projections collapsed. In return, Musk taunted the short sellers by selling Tesla-branded "short shorts" with "S3XY" emblazoned on the back. Though Musk himself once tweeted that the stock price was "too high imo", it went on defying gravity, and by the end of 2021, Tesla short sellers had collectively lost US$28.5 billion.

Some hardened Wall Streeters admitted it was the most wrong they had ever been. "You have to be careful not to let yourself be triggered by Mr. Musk," the veteran hedge funder George Noble told *New York Magazine*. "The outright lies, the violation of laws – you just want to punch the guy out, but you have to resist the temptation." He blamed "a post-truth society" for the company's wacky valuations, and "stupid dumbfuck millennial investors who don't know how to read income statements and balance sheets". Investors had gone to the extreme of flying drones over Tesla factories to ascertain production numbers in real time, and it had made no difference. They marvelled at Musk's ability to avoid repercussions, especially from government bodies. He seemed to have "regulatory immunity", as one of them put it.

Musk and his superfans have not forgotten the atmosphere of existential threat

The short sellers lost, the media coverage was mostly fawning, and after years of analyst attacks over its balance sheets, Tesla became the most profitable company in the United States (a Tesla car was even modified into a coal roller). Still, Musk and his superfans have not forgotten the atmosphere of existential threat. They forged bonds that were material as well as psychological. Musk has the ability to shift markets with a single tweet or statement, and his jokes and memes are purposed this way too, sometimes into coded phrases. When he championed the tongue-in-cheek cryptocurrency Dogecoin ("The most entertaining outcome and the most ironic outcome would be that dogecoin becomes the currency of Earth in the future," he wrote) he also pumped its value, leading to a US$258 billion lawsuit accusing him of manipulation.

No medium is better suited to this CEO-as-rebel pose than algorithmically driven, for-profit social media. Its immediacy is unmatched by any pre-digital medium. Some argue it is closer to oral traditions than literate ones, more like talking than writing ("Orality is participatory, interactive, communal and focused on the present. The Web is all of these things," as design instructor Irwin Chen put it). The biggest accounts on social media, which have audiences in the hundreds of millions, enjoy a broadcast power that far outstrips radio or television. Musk's replies to other people's tweets are frequent and brief ("interesting" or "concerning" are some of his favourites), and can bring an account to the attention of an audience multi-millions strong.

This also means Musk's own Twitter activity is closely observed for auspices and hints. Careful attention is paid to whom he follows and unfollows, who is in favour or out of it (when he unfollowed the journalist Matt Taibbi, for example, it made national news). A University of Washington study of influential Twitter accounts at the outbreak of the Israel–Hamas war in October 2023 identified a "new elite" of formerly obscure accounts like @visegrad24 and @CensoredMen, which had more influence than traditional news sources like CNN and the BBC. "One key to the surging popularity of these accounts might be Musk himself," the report concluded. "Through following many of these accounts, replying to them, and directly recommending them, Musk may be playing a significant role in the increasing prominence of these news-focused sources."

Donald Trump pioneered this algorithmic approach to public life. Social media was not only his means for ascending to the presidency of the United States; it was the only way such a rise became possible. Beforehand, the legacy media could still end or inhibit a political career on character grounds, and only weak counterattacks were available: press releases, lawsuits, half-ignored public appearances. That has changed. The Musk/Trump comparison is often made – both are transformative figures able to resist moral judgement from mainstream sources. In the *New Republic*, Alex Shephard argued that "Musk has, over the past year, done his best to occupy the role that Donald Trump did before he was suspended from the platform ... He is Twitter's perennial main character, whose antics set the day's agenda." He, too, is "a divisive presence".

Musk reportedly dislikes Trump and has called him a "bullshitter" (in return, Trump has called him a "bullshit artist"). Musk was among the executives selected as business advisers to the 45th president, a fraught role he accepted with reluctance. He had been critical of Trump's candidacy – he thought it reduced America's standing in the world – and kept expressing these reservations once Trump assumed office. It was a moral quandary. Musk was then opposed to Trump's climate and immigration policies, and wanted to be a critical voice who still had the president's ear. But once Trump withdrew the United States from the Paris Climate Accords, Musk realised his position had become untenable and resigned.

This Musk – the voice of liberal reason, operating deep in enemy territory – already feels like a man from another era. Trump has changed Musk more than vice-versa. The discourse licensed by the former president, the vituperative name-calling and abuse of public enemies, has added a harder edge to Musk's trolling. Such is the tenor of the time. When Trump and DeSantis fans began to clash online in earnest, anticipating the pair's contest in the presidential primaries, they traded accusations of paedophilia (in the form of "grooming") for both candidates, a charge that has become common on the right side of US politics.

These abrasive public exchanges show that obnoxious right-wing public figures are a demand-driven phenomenon. And the demand is greater than the supply. In the United States, very few A-list celebrities are outspoken conservatives. The actors Clint Eastwood, Mel Gibson, Jon Voight and James Woods still have genuine cachet, but then the drop-off in name recognition is steep. Ted Nugent, Aaron Carter, Kid Rock and Stephen Baldwin got top billing among those endorsing Donald Trump in 2016; the biggest celebrity to attend Trump's 2017 inauguration was the former *Happy Days* star Scott Baio (coincidentally, Voight and Baio were co-stars in *Superbabies: Baby Geniuses 2*). And Eastwood was a Mike Pence man.

There are similarly slim pickings in the business world. Despite Trump's big-business pedigree, his election was a rebuke to free marketeers and Chamber of Commerce Republicans, and most of his political donations came from individuals offering small sums. Traditional conservative mega-donors like the Koch brothers were among the most dedicated anti-Trumpers. Peter Thiel's interest in Trumpworld has waned, and he wound up disappointed in the administration. The most notable exception has been the MyPillow founder Mike Lindell, who played a cameo role in efforts to overturn the result of the 2020 election.

All this makes the cultural leadership of American conservatism surprisingly thin. The most decorated captains in the culture war tend to be conservative media figures with an online audience. Religious figures have lost their clout, and even Fox News has struggled to keep pace: Tucker Carlson's firing and Sean Hannity's diminished ratings saw influence ebb away from what had been a king-making institution. The conservative Catholic commentator Sohrab Ahmari complained that right populism, once touted as the future of the Republican Party, had instead turned into a "niche/trashy online-media product" that draws huge numbers of eyeballs but was "less and less a credible political force".

Republicans in the United States have an unsatiated hunger for allies with real-world gravitas, who make money or mainstream movies or content at scale. They are desperate enough that almost anyone can gain their trust. Theirs is a milieu where one-time dating coaches, failed actors and former beauty queens are commonplace (the prominent right-wingers Candace Owens, Scott Presler, Tomi Lahren and Lauren Boebert, for example, are all one-time clients of a single talent agency). If these wannabes can reach an audience of millions, a genuinely famous business figure can unlock more power still. Trump did it and now Musk is doing it too. This switch in political affiliation carries immediate and extraordinary rewards that outweigh the penalties.

Musk's huge and dedicated audience can also be used as a weapon

There have been legislative perks: in June 2023, when Governor DeSantis banned direct-to-consumer car sales in Florida (a sop to car dealerships, an important Republican constituency), Tesla and other EV manufacturers were exempted. But the most valuable dividends are cultural. By May 2023, a Morning Consult poll found that Musk had become the most popular political figure in the United States, pipping Trump and Biden. The postures he struck – pro free speech, personally combative, socially liberal but anti-woke – had strong appeal to the American public. His new fans were vociferous, loyal and now had the same set of enemies that he did.

Musk's huge and dedicated audience, big enough to make @CensoredMen bigger than CNN, can also be used as a weapon. The practice of setting a social media fanbase onto an individual target is called "brigading", and Musk has some of the most feared brigades on the internet. "Musk's tweets to his tens of millions of followers have for years prompted his supporters to deluge the targets of his ire with online threats," the *Washington Post* reported. When Missy Cummings, a self-driving sceptic, was appointed to an important automotive regulatory body, Musk and his fans went after her publicly until at least one death threat was investigated by North Carolina police. Musk's campaign against Twitter's former head of trust and safety, Yoel Roth, became so extreme that Roth had to sell his house and relocate. "Musk appeared to endorse a tweet that baselessly accused Roth of being sympathetic to pedophilia," CNN reported, "a common trope used by conspiracy theorists to attack people online."

Those closest to Musk speak of him entering a "demon mode" characterised by high energy and low empathy. His white-collar workplaces can be casually abusive; his blue-collar factories and plants were investigated for racial and sexual harassment. Tesla factories are renowned for having the highest injury rates in the car industry. He flouted Covid regulations, and thwarted health and safety investigations. His launch sites pumped millions of gallons of wastewater into neighbouring wetlands. Such are the costs of doing business when nothing can interfere with the mission. By the time Musk came to purchase Twitter, ruthless firings and stringent conditions were expected. But the purchase itself was also the purchase of an army: "demon mode" made legion.

Buying Twitter

Why did Elon Musk purchase Twitter? Unlike his other businesses, the social media platform has no obvious connection to his mission (which Grimes, on Twitter, summarised as "Sustainable energy, making humanity a multiplanetary species and the preservation of consciousness"). For his whole career, Musk had specialised in start-up companies that promise new products and services. Twitter, by contrast, was not just a mature public company, but an entrenched cultural phenomenon that had been around for more than fifteen years. Musk himself was hesitant, trying to pull out of the purchase, and with good reason. To date, buying the social media platform was not only his worst business decision but, in dollar terms, arguably one of the worst business decisions anyone has ever made.

It took just a few months of Musk's ownership of the company to lose an estimated two-thirds of its US$44 billion purchase price. His distracted and erratic leadership also cost Tesla. The car company's losses were led by poor forecasts for the outlandish Cybertruck, a retro-futuristic wedge of stainless steel that drew comparisons to *Mad Max* and the DeLorean. After years-long cycles of hype and delay, the vehicle arrived, only to "dig its own grave", in Musk's own phrasing. In the disastrous earnings call that followed, one anonymous investor crowed that Musk had behaved like a "little baby" who was "almost in tears". Over a thirteen-month period, his net worth declined by US$200 billion, roughly the value of Ukraine's gross domestic product, followed by a US$13 billion loss in a single April day. This turbulence has a possible root cause: a comedy website getting into trouble.

The Babylon Bee, known to its fans as the Bee, is a US-based Christian humour site with a sizeable following, a kind of anti-woke version of the satirical news outfit The Onion. Musk had previously fanboyed over The Onion, which he called "the greatest publication in the history of all conscious beings, living or dead", admiring it so much that he emailed its staff about his favourite jokes. He even weighed up acquiring the site, and when two senior Onion editors left to pursue ambitious real-world satire projects (one involved building an "entire museum wing imagining Britain's imperialist conquest of Heaven"), Musk gave them US$2 million. Together, the three of them launched Thud!, a "new intergalactic media empire, exclamation point optional", Musk tweeted. Tongue in cheek, he told the Daily Beast it was "pretty obvious that comedy is the next frontier after electric vehicles, space exploration, and brain-computer interfaces ... Don't know how anyone's not seeing this." After concern that Thud!'s jokes could interfere with SpaceX's business (his drug tests for the 420 joke seemed to be front of mind), he walked back the project's funding.

There were no hard feelings with the editors of Thud!, but when the remaining Onion team began teasing Musk, it rankled. "Elon Musk Insists He'd Be Much More Innovative Pedophile Than Thailand Rescue Worker", read one headline. But the joke that stung most was a single word, which ran in a feature called "The Richest Person in Every State and How They Made Their Money". Under Musk's name it said only "apartheid", a rather unfair reference to his father's business interests. Musk was furious. "Shame on you, Onion," he tweeted in response on 26 March 2021. "This is why people are switching to @TheBabylonBee!" He unfollowed The Onion's official account around the same time.

The Babylon Bee leaned into the attention. Its headlines about Musk were fawning instead of barbed, painting him as a heroic rocketeer ("Elon Musk Rescues Texans with Giant Flamethrower Mech"). He promoted them in turn. Almost one year after Musk's break-up with The Onion, in March 2022, the Bee named US Assistant Secretary for Health Rachel Levine as its "Man of the Year". Levine is trans, and the award was a signature example of the Bee's predictable brand of comedy, except this time it resulted in the immediate suspension of the Babylon Bee's account by Twitter. Deliberately misgendering someone is a violation of the platform's hateful conduct policy. Or, at least, it was.

Thanks to court filings, a rare blow-by-blow chronology of what happened next later become public. In response to the Bee's banning, one of Elon Musk's contacts named "TJ" texted him straight away: "Can you buy Twitter and then delete it, please!? xx America is going INSANE." Court filings revealed that "TJ" was Musk's ex-wife Talulah Riley, who had been angered by the Bee's fate. "The Babylon Bee got suspension is crazy. Raiyah and I were talking about it today. It was a fucking joke," she continued. "Why has everyone become so puritanical?" ("Raiyah" is Princess Raiyah bint Al Hussein, of Jordan, daughter of the American-born Queen Noor of Jordan and one of Riley's confidantes.) "Or can you buy Twitter and make it radically free-speech?" Riley texted Musk. "So much stupidity comes from Twitter xx."

> *Content-moderation issues had provoked him into a takeover, hostile if necessary*

Riley's idea took hold. Almost immediately, Musk reached out to Seth Dillon, the Babylon Bee's CEO. First, Musk confirmed that the Bee's suspension was real (it was). Almost the next day, on 25 March, Musk rolled out a poll to his millions of Twitter followers. "Free speech is essential to a functioning democracy," he wrote. "Do you believe Twitter rigorously adheres to this principle?" The result was a resounding no. In a follow-up tweet Musk emphasised that "the consequences of this poll will be important". Ten days later, on 4 April, he announced himself as the site's largest shareholder, with a 9 per cent stake. There was already an acquisition plan in place for the rest. Content-moderation issues had provoked him into a takeover, hostile if necessary.

This was a shock to the site's incumbent owners, who found themselves in the crosshairs of the world's richest man. Musk and Twitter's CEO, Parag Agrawal, began a tense pas de deux, much of it played out on Twitter itself. When a board seat was presented to Musk as a peace offering, he rejected it. Musk then got cold feet, and tried to back out of the deal, but it was too late. The number of fake Twitter accounts became a sticking point or possible get-out clause: Musk claimed there were so many it made the site's valuation fraudulent, and sought evidence from specialist disinformation analysts to make his case. Agrawal countered these charges in a stream of tweets. Musk responded with the poop emoji (💩). It was to become a recurring motif in what followed.

In time, Musk's offer became irrefutable, the board caved and the fake-accounts question became a legal matter. Finally, on 26 October 2022, Musk arrived at Twitter's California headquarters in a black t-shirt and black pants, brandishing a white ceramic kitchen sink in both hands. The "Meme Lord" arriving at Twitter HQ as a real live meme was carrying an eye-rolling visual pun. "Let that sink in!" was his caption, as he uploaded a video of his visit. Twitter had become a private company in the sole ownership of proprietor Elon Musk, and he had paid US$44 billion for the pleasure. His vision, he said, was that one billion people per day would use the site (it then had an engaged audience of around a quarter of a billion). There was subtext just as unsubtle as the joke: Musk was going to throw the kitchen sink at them. The *Washington Post* was already reporting plans to fire 75 per cent of Twitter's staff. He began the bloodletting by firing Agrawal.

As soon as Musk's ownership was announced, several advertisers paused their ad spends, worried by the site's new direction. They were also spooked by Musk coming to the defence of *Dilbert* cartoonist Scott Adams. In a video posted online, Adams had advised white people "to get the hell away from Black people", among other racist sentiments, and as a result of this call for segregation, his cartoons were dropped by every major newspaper in the country. Book plans with Penguin Random House were cancelled, and he was fired by his distributor. In a tweet, Musk claimed that this shunning showed it was the media who were racist, not Adams. They were "racist against whites & Asians", and elite colleges were the same.

In the United States, there is a half-century-old tradition of treating neo-Nazism as a limit case for the protections of the First Amendment, as well as a stress test for reasoned debate, free speech and intellectual enquiry. In 1966 the country's leading neo-Nazi, George Lincoln Rockwell, was an invited speaker at Brown University, where lecture attendees gave him a polite if strained reception. A decade later, a planned demonstration by white nationalists in Skokie, Illinois (where almost half the residents were Jewish), became famous as a legal landmark after being blocked by officials. The American Civil Liberties Union, arguing on the Nazis' behalf, persuaded the Supreme Court of the group's right to hold the rally; its Jewish lawyer, David Goldberger, was threatened with baseball bats. As many as 50,000 ACLU members resigned, but the principle held and was widely copied, though the ACLU has since diluted its position, especially after the white nationalist march at Charlottesville, Virginia, in 2017.

The most charitable explanation for Musk's Twitter takeover is that he saw himself as part of the same tradition. "By 'free speech'," he tweeted on 27 April 2022, "I simply mean that which matches the law. I am against censorship that goes far beyond the law. If people want less free speech, they will ask government to pass laws to that effect. Therefore, going beyond the law is contrary to the will of the people." This received almost 800,000 likes. It was a defensible position with a glaring oversight: Twitter was a for-profit venture, not a soapbox. No other commercial ventures online used the First Amendment as their sole moderation policy, and for good reason. Paring back moderation to what was legal might allow, for example, computer-generated child pornography on the site (a 2002 US Supreme Court case found that it was protected speech). Likewise, so-called gore videos, which depict real-life instances of torture, executions or fatal accidents, do not violate America's federal obscenity statutes. On other major social media platforms like Facebook, the unfortunate staff who moderate these materials sometimes develop post-traumatic stress disorder.

Even the National Coalition Against Censorship noted that obscenity laws only apply to sexually oriented materials and "there is interestingly no limit to the amount of simulated or real violence that can be viewed", but thought publishing such material was an act of individual conscience. Was Musk's Twitter really going to allow all this? The few sites on the internet that did publish such material struggled to stay online: they tended to be blackballed by vital tech infrastructure partners. In part, social media platforms have moderated hateful content because they have no viable alternative. Sites that abandon moderation altogether become infested with Nazis, or paedophiles, or both (sometimes deliberately so in the case of the social media platform Gab), and only fellow corporations can apply accountability. After the 2018 Tree of Life synagogue shooting in Pittsburgh, Pennsylvania, most of the companies that processed Gab's donations and hosted its web presence withdrew their services – the site spent a year offline.

The web security provider Cloudflare, which has similar free speech bona fides to Musk, initially provided services to the neo-Nazi site the Daily Stormer, along with trolling and harassment sites 8chan and Kiwi Farms. Eventually, Cloudflare dropped the sites after they were implicated in harassment campaigns, mass shootings, suicides, "doxxing" (releasing individuals' private information and home addresses online) and "swatting" (calling in false police reports that result in armed tactical law enforcement units being sent to a target's home). Cloudflare was scarred by the experience: it resisted pressure to stop providing services to Kiwi Farms for years before suddenly dropping the site, pointing to an "imminent threat to human life". Regulating such material, it concluded, was not its role and should be conducted by the government.

> *He called his plan "freedom of speech, not freedom of reach"*

On Twitter, allowing similarly legal but objectionable material would be commercial suicide. In a private email thread, the Colgate-Palmolive VP Diana Haussling said she was a "huge supporter of free speech" but that no firm would "ignore the impact of such hate speech", and that she couldn't ignore it as a Black woman. The chief marketing officer of McDonald's characterised Twitter post-acquisition as lurching from "chaos to moments of irresponsibility". Months after the purchase, Musk appeared at a major marketing conference to make a direct appeal to advertisers to return, but few bought his pitch. The conference did have one fringe benefit:

he ended up hiring his on-stage interlocutor, NBCUniversal ad chief Linda Yaccarino, as Twitter's next CEO. It was not an easy job.

Ordinarily, Musk's fortune could just absorb the losses, but his Twitter purchase was funded in part by private equity, which expected immediate cashflow in return. If the pre-takeover, moderated version of Twitter did not clear a profit, how could a free-for-all that repelled advertisers expect to do any better? Musk's plan was drastic. First, he would cut costs by firing three-quarters of Twitter's staff. Then he would make up the advertising shortfall – which he hoped would be temporary – by charging premium users US$8 each per month. This would also solve part of the moderation problem. "The propensity of someone to engage in hate speech if they've paid $8 and are risking their account," he said. "Think about it ... how much hate speech do you encounter if you're at a party, or at an event?"

It was an idea that had already failed elsewhere. While it made intuitive sense that internet users wouldn't post abuse under their own names, years of bitter experience suggested otherwise. Jaded forum moderators and Facebook group admins everywhere knew that the effect of anonymity on internet abuse could be trivial or non-existent. Major studies demonstrated the same thing. Researchers at the University of Zurich found anonymous users were *less* likely to post abuse than people using their real names, perhaps because abusers were seeking peer approval. Still, Musk had a back-up plan: instead of hate speech being banned outright, it would be suppressed by the site's algorithm. He called it "freedom of speech, not freedom of reach". Implementing the policy was the hard part – most of the site's moderation staff had resigned or been fired.

Musk had a particular resentment towards these people, especially the independent Trust and Safety Council that the old Twitter had assembled. Described by Reuters as "comprised of various civil rights organizations, academics and other bodies that advocated for safety and advised Twitter as it developed products, programs, and rules", the council, Musk seemed to suggest, should be criminally prosecuted for refusing to take action on child exploitation. He promptly dissolved it. While sorting through Twitter's offices, he found a closet full of t-shirts sporting the phrase #StayWoke. He tweeted a video of the discovery: here was Exhibit A of the censorious mindset and political bias he had long alleged. A brief détente between Musk and the site's senior security and privacy executives ended with more mass firings. This development attracted the attention of a federal regulator – the Federal Trade Commission (FTC) expressed its "deep concern".

Prior to Musk's takeover, Twitter had been repeatedly investigated by the FTC for misleading users over privacy, in 2011 the FTC had required Twitter to file compulsory reports about its improvements. The site had already violated this order, resulting in a stiff US$150 million settlement in 2022. How, the FTC wondered, could Twitter maintain its users' privacy with no privacy staff? Across the EU, which had just passed the sweeping *Digital Services Act*, the warnings were more dire: if Twitter did not comply with its rules around disinformation, targeted advertising and illegal content, it could face billions of euros in fines, or even an outright ban.

Musk was used to overriding oversight. The Securities and Exchange Commission (SEC) had done little to him: after attempting to ban him for life from running a public company, it settled for a US$20 million fine for misleading investors on Twitter. ("I do not respect the SEC. I do not respect them," Musk told *60 Minutes* afterwards.) The Federal Aviation Authority had reprimanded him, but declined to fine him, stating publicly that there was no point because he had too much money. Twitter had a different kind of exposure. Regulators in the United States and Europe were eyeing it closely, and not only were the fines heavier, but the reputational penalties could also scare away advertisers who already looked jittery.

Musk began sleeping in the Twitter offices, just as he had back in his dotcom start-up beginnings. Esther Crawford, a senior Twitter employee, did so too as a show of fealty, tweeting a photo of herself with an eye mask on, wrapped in a silver sleeping bag, lying on the floor next to a bank of executive chairs. Recognising her new boss's tastes, she also sent him edgy memes late at night. Four months later she was fired after raising internal concerns (she found out when her laptop stopped working). Recounting her experience to the writer Ben Mezrich, she said that Musk was maybe the saddest, loneliest man she'd ever met.

Crawford had tried to prevent one of Musk's most damaging management decisions. He had, he said, lit on a way to attract user payments. For US$8 a month, anyone could get the same blue checkmarks previously reserved for "verified" Twitter accounts, those held by corporations, celebrities and reporters. In some corners of the internet, the phrase "blue checks" was used as a pejorative – a shorthand for the insular, self-satisfied priest class of the mainstream media. Musk announced those legacy checkmarks would be stripped. The business case was slim, and he did little to disguise that it was also an act of revenge, striking a blow against the moralisers, critics and wokerati. Though his targets did get upset – the *New York Times* called it "Blue Check Apocalypse" – Crawford's predictions about an impersonation crisis came true. A fake official Nintendo account published a picture of Mario giving the finger. "Coca-Cola" announced cocaine was being added to the formula again.

Musk found the chaos funny, though panicked calls from sales and marketing persuaded him to put it to a halt. He was applying his old iterative approach – trial and error, slash and burn, in-jokes and demon mode – but this was different. With moderation pared back, the site was becoming radioactive for advertisers. Users scrolling through videos might suddenly encounter an arguing couple fall from a collapsing balcony. Twitter failed to detect footage from the Christchurch massacre being circulated, and it was only removed after the New Zealand government notified the company. Searches for "dog" autocompleted to "dog stabbed with a screwdriver", offering footage of a Staffordshire terrier being stabbed in the eye during a burglary. "Cat" became "cat in a blender",

> *Musk threw a troll party, with himself as the guest of honour*

and seemed to show a kitten being killed. A London mother, Laura Clemons, contacted Twitter to warn them and received no response; when a news organisation took up her case, the Twitter press department responded with the poop emoji. By then it had become the company's default response to media enquiries. Certain accounts – some with large followings – posted Hollywood films in their entirety, sometimes with the precursor "fuck it". That attitude prevailed.

Musk was finding out the hard way that Twitter was a culture as much as a company. It might have been a culture he hated, but it held millions of users and ad dollars together. His quick-fire attempts to change it had something sadistic and retaliatory to them – Crawford could sense real anger under the jokes. Better leadership would have projected calm while moderation was thin. Instead, Musk threw a troll party, with himself as the guest of honour. Not only did some of the world's worst people avail themselves of the new blue checks (the Premium subscription meant their replies were boosted too), but Musk also announced an amnesty for banned accounts. The most famous was Donald Trump, who had been banned, controversially, for inciting violence before and during the attempted insurrection on 6 January 2021. Though his Twitter account was reinstated in late November 2022, Trump stayed on his own social media platform, Truth Social, and did not resume tweeting.

But others did. Hours after Musk's purchase was finalised, "a specific racist epithet used to demean Black people shot up by 500%", a Center for Countering Digital Hate report found, the result of a trolling campaign testing the site's new limits. Kanye West returned, fresh from an antisemitism scandal that had ended a billion-dollar relationship with Adidas; his first tweet back was "Shalom :)" The campaign manager for West's presidential campaign, Holocaust denier Nick Fuentes, also returned, a week after calling Hitler "really fucking cool". So did Andrew Anglin, founder of the Daily Stormer, days after a Montana judge issued a bench warrant for his arrest – he owed US$14 million to victims of racist harassment campaigns he had coordinated. "Saying you love Hitler is no big deal," he tweeted on his first day back. "No one cares about that. The man died 80 years ago."

Also returning was the white nationalist and antisemite Tim Gionet, known as Baked Alaska, who would shortly be imprisoned for his role in the January 6 uprising. A few weeks before, Musk had tweeted a photo of Gionet saluting a McDonald's flag flying at half-mast, and then deleted it. Gionet tweeted: "5 years ago I was banned on Twitter. Today I am back. All glory to God. Thank you Elon Musk for giving me another chance." Ali Alexander was there, another Capitol riot alumnus, who believed Jews could travel through time. He tweeted: "The Enemy made false promises to our opponents. Their murderous lust for our destruction made them greedy. As a result, they've destroyed faith in already failing institutions and forced Twitter to go private. Normalizing us. Thank you @elonmusk. Now, bring everyone else." E. Michael Jones celebrated his return with this tweet: "My prayer for the beginning of 2023 is that God will bring about a peaceful end to the American empire. I also pray that during 2023 God will break the yoke of Jewish tyranny which oppresses us." Some, such as Alexander and Fuentes, were quickly banned again. Other stayed.

The amnesty fitted Musk's approach to free speech. But this was something different from a gritty, Voltaire-style commitment to principle. Musk not only allowed notorious antisemites back onto the platform – he welcomed them with open arms, sometimes personally. At first the contacts seemed to be circumstantial. Musk might tweet memes or images associated with white nationalist accounts – the character Pepe the Frog, for example – deleting them when told of their provenance. Then the flirtations became more overt: Musk was "engaging with far-right personalities, recycling their tropes, and entertaining their grievances", as one researcher put it. It looked more like a meeting of minds than the principled support of unpopular speech.

Musk publicly tweeted at right-wing journalist Elijah Schaffer several times, checking his experience of the new Twitter: "Are you still finding engagement to be low?" "If bots are removed from the system, their likes will be removed too. Are you seeing likes from clearly human accounts disappear?" Schaffer had been fired from The Blaze, a conservative media site founded by Glenn Beck, after repeated allegations of sexual harassment and assault, and with this red-carpet welcome on Twitter, he began testing his reach. On 25 March he tweeted out a poll: "Did the good guys win WWII?"

The result: 42 per cent of more than 100,000 voted No. He tried again: "Do you believe Jews disproportionately control the world institutions, banks, & are waging a war on white, western society?" More than 70 per cent of respondents believed the answer was "Yes, 100%" or "Yes, it's complicated". The poll received more than 94,000 votes, and 1.8 million views.

Musk had declared peace with the white nationalist trolls. He sent laughing emojis to Andrew Torba, head of Gab. An account named @TopLobsta posted a picture comparing Joe Biden with a buff Mel Gibson, sporting the caption "You can do adrenochrome or you can hate the Js. Which Way Western Man?" The Js here means Jews, and "adrenochrome" refers to a conspiracy theory retread of blood libel, where celebrities and politicians supposedly drink the blood of tortured children. "Gibson is really that buff these days?" Musk responded. No one so chronically online could be unfamiliar with the widespread white supremacist shorthand, and @TopLobsta's reply removed any ambiguity. It was a workout routine for Gibson: "3×10 ADL reprimandation 5×5 holocaust denials 7×3 rabbi bashing".

Musk had been defended by some Jewish organisations after comparing perennial target of antisemites George Soros to the supervillain Magneto (both are Holocaust survivors). But now the coincidences were racking up, as were the criticisms. This left Musk with a needle to thread. He had empowered previously banned racists, but he also needed to claim Twitter's hate speech metrics were going down. The Center for Countering Digital Hate's report showed that "the number of tweets containing slurs is far higher under Musk". Instead of counting the incidence of slurs – the methodology that Twitter itself used – Musk counted impressions, the number of times each slur was seen. "Hate speech impressions continue to decline, despite significant user growth!", he stated. He suspended the accounts of reporters who criticised him, including the *Washington Post*'s Taylor Lorenz, then reinstated them after running a poll. He labelled National Public Radio "US state-affiliated media", then changed his mind after a conversation with Walter Isaacson.

The First Amendment also affirms the right to freedom of association. A private social media company banning someone from posting is also protected by it, for example. And the alternative – that government compels a company to publish political opinions – has obvious free speech implications of a different kind. Musk was free to allow hate speech on Twitter, and advertisers were free to stay away. But he would not accept this outcome, or the chain of causation that led up to it. Instead, someone must be to blame. And this time, instead of the government, or regulations, or the "woke mind virus", it would be the Jews themselves.

> **Musk was free to allow hate speech on Twitter, and advertisers were free to stay away**

#BANTHEADL

Back when Elon Musk was finalising his takeover of Twitter, anti-racism organisations expressed their misgivings. Some made public condemnations, or began campaigns of action and persuasion. The Anti-Defamation League opted for a more lateral strategy: it decided to try flattery. "Elon Musk is an amazing entrepreneur and extraordinary innovator," the ADL head, Jonathan Greenblatt, told an interviewer on CNBC's *Squawk Box*, only to finish with a bizarre flourish: "He is the Henry Ford of our time."

Name-checking one of the most famous antisemites of the twentieth century – author and publisher of *The International Jew*, a hater of such influence that a large photo of Ford was kept in Hitler's office – was an odd touch, almost a Freudian slip. Greenblatt retracted his jarring statement as soon as he was off-air. It was "flat-out wrong", he said; he only meant that he was excited, and, having met Musk several times, was looking forward to his innovations in the public square.

If this was reverse psychology, it backfired: before a year passed, the League would have armed guards posted outside its headquarters, while in Florida masked men marched, waving Nazi flags and chanting "Ban the ADL". It was a phrase Musk himself had helped to popularise.

By 2023, hate speech and antisemitism on the new-look Twitter were causing serious alarm. More than 100 Jewish organisations and groups had signed an open letter to Musk denouncing it; Elad Nehorai noted in *Forward* that Musk "consistently finds himself chatting it up with Twitter's best-known antisemites" and that his ownership of the platform made him "the loudest, and most powerful antisemite in American history". The best empirical evidence suggested that his "freedom of speech, not freedom of reach" approach for hate speech was failing. One think tank, the Institute for Strategic Dialogue, showed that antisemitic speech had doubled since his takeover, and that what it termed "hateful account creation" had surged. Contrary to Musk's statement that there were fewer impressions of such material, the ISD found "only a very small decrease in the average levels of engagement".

Musk had promised to make many mistakes after taking over Twitter, using the same approach he had taken at Tesla and SpaceX. Moving fast and breaking things had worked while the companies were young and focused on engineering prototypes, but Twitter was a mature enterprise, with a platform culture that had been adjusted over a decade and a half. It was reliant on advertising, not sales. Musk first tried to change this by diversifying Twitter's revenue. Content creators got a share of advertising revenue, a strategy aimed at taking on YouTube. Musk wanted subscription revenue to be around half the site's turnover, but by February 2023, estimates put the new blue-check programme at 300,000 sign-ups, only around 0.12 per cent of active users. Advertising, meanwhile, was at a fraction of what it once was.

It was under these clouds that Linda Yaccarino, Twitter's CEO since May 2023, suggested a meeting with Greenblatt to clear the air. The appointment of Yaccarino, one of the most advertising-savvy media executives in the country, was widely understood as an attempt to draw major advertisers back to Twitter. So many had left that Musk sometimes took to praising the remaining ones personally on the site. Chief among these firms' concerns was "brand safety", which meant not appearing alongside extremist content. On Twitter this was now a problem. Advertising for both the FIFA Women's World Cup and *Sports Illustrated*, for example, had run on a pro-Hitler account undetected.

Greenblatt knew that major changes were unlikely – Twitter's moderation policies were set by Musk – but he at least wanted to prosecute his case, which centred on incitement rather than hate speech. Musk, meanwhile, was infuriated by any suggestion that hate speech had increased since his takeover. He had admonished a BBC reporter for suggesting as much, called the Institute for Strategic Dialogue report "nonsense" and sued the Center for Countering Digital Hate, which had collated examples. He had already singled out the Anti-Defamation League's criticisms, once posting that it should instead be named the "Defamation League". Whatever the outcome of the meeting between Greenblatt and Yaccarino, Musk looked determined to undermine it.

After Greenblatt tweeted that the meeting had been "candid and productive", there was a swirl of activity, on both Twitter and other platforms such as the messaging service Telegram. A campaign began, boosted by Nick Fuentes and "Keith Woods", the pseudonym of the Irish white nationalist and National Party member Keith O'Brien. Woods was a self-confessed antisemite and Holocaust denier, and an associate of not only Fuentes but also the well-known neo-Nazi Richard Spencer. Their campaign was coordinated around a hashtag: #BanTheADL, a call for the organisation to be purged from Twitter. Between 4 and 13 September, Twitter Premium subscribers tweeted the hashtag at least 37,471 times. Musk, who was by then interacting with Woods openly and in person, began promoting it too.

"ADL has tried very hard to strangle X/Twitter," Musk wrote in one reply, calling the organisation one of "the biggest generators of anti-Semitism on this platform". For the neo-Nazis it was better than Christmas. Fuentes crowed that the material was getting into the mainstream: "everywhere you look, people are now talking about the Jews". He credited their "audience of one. Elon Musk is paying attention". The veteran tech writer Walt Mossberg deactivated his Twitter account in disgust, citing the campaign and the "delight of antisemites and other haters".

The ADL tried to hold its ground against this Musk-led onslaught of trolling. It was "unsurprised yet undeterred that antisemites, white supremacists, conspiracy theorists and other trolls have launched a coordinated attack on our organization", Greenblatt said in a statement. "Such insidious efforts don't daunt us. Instead, they drive us to be unflinching in our commitment to fight hate in all its forms and ensure the safety of Jewish communities and other marginalized groups." In response, Musk suggested he might sue the ADL for US$22 billion, blaming the organisation for pressuring advertisers and causing Twitter to lose billions in value over the past six months. This was useful cover. Sources at multiple advertising industry firms who had recommended pausing major campaigns told the site Marketing Brew that activist groups had "not played a role in their decisions regarding advertising spend on Twitter". Musk's volatility, not activist pressure, had led to the exodus.

Before Musk's takeover, the site had been losing US$4 million a day, a scale of loss typical of the VC-fuelled, growth-centred practices of Silicon Valley. That negative cashflow was now coupled with devaluation. Even the decision to rebrand the company as "X" did serious damage, wiping billions in brand recognition value. The ugly and bruising attacks on the ADL did little to help. The ADL was far from a flawless organisation, but any substantive debate about free speech or moderation was buried in an avalanche of trolling. Those leading the attack on the ADL – and being boosted by Musk – cared about hate speech, not free speech. They disliked the ADL because it represented Jews, and they hated Jews and said so.

> *The decision to rebrand the company as "X" did serious damage, wiping billions in brand recognition value*

Surveying the damage, Musk went on a ludicrous and humiliating damage-control tour. "In some respects I think I am Jewish, basically," he told the conservative Jewish media figure Ben Shapiro. He met with Benjamin Netanyahu. He called himself "aspirationally Jewish" and "pro-Semitic", and made statements opposing antisemitism ("To be super clear, I'm pro free speech, but against anti-Semitism of any kind"). He was, he said, aware that people would cite their "Jewish friend" in this situation, but he had *friends*, plural. Anyway, his Jewish biographer, Walter Isaacson, had detected no hatred of Jews in the years he'd spent with his subject, so that was surely definitive.

Not all trolls are antisemites, but virtually all antisemites are trolls. Indefatigable, sadistic, ever-present, primed any hour of the day or night: internet trolls are some of the few beings on the same wavelength as Musk. Already simpatico, they were also grateful for the amnesty he granted them. A constant theme in Musk's professional life is his intensity, which is seldom matched by others. Arianna Huffington once wrote an open letter in the *New York Times* imploring him to have more rest, thereby setting a better example for other executives. He replied that Ford and Tesla were the only two American car companies to have avoided bankruptcy. Rest was not an option. As the purchase of Twitter was finalised, he played the console game *Elden Ring* until 5.30 am, unable to sleep.

The neo-Nazis and anti-vaxxers he allowed back to the site would act as his shock troops, a kind of penal battalion of the banned. His pardon has bought their loyalty. They are ready to prosecute his interests for free, sometimes even paying for the privilege, consummating the relationship between the authoritarian leader and authoritarian follower. They match his vindictiveness and apply it to the same targets. They're having a similar type of fun. More critical than his mindset is his reach – and with 165 million followers on Twitter, his reach is extraordinary. The worst of his fan base take aim at a common enemy on his behalf: the same moralisers and regulators, the government, media, activists and NGOs.

At another time, even a recent time, Musk's flirtations might have imperilled his career and social standing. But the social penalty for consorting with neo-Nazis has lately been much reduced. Donald Trump had already dined with Nick Fuentes in November 2022, when he was a guest at Mar-a-Lago (Trump claimed not to know who he was, and that he was there only as an invitee of the rapper Kanye West, recently disgraced for his own antisemitic comments). The Republican congresswoman Marjorie Taylor Greene spoke at a Fuentes-led conference, with no consequences.

Perhaps Musk had decided racist trolls could be of use to the mission, and bet that the stigma around them was declining. His fanbase, both the rusted-on Tesla fanatics and the trolls welcomed back to Twitter, would see him through. Morality would ultimately be determined by the mission, not the media. The truly sinful are those unbelievers who stand in the way of ascension (this time to Mars). Musk had also been prepared for accusations around hate speech to become a major issue once he took over Twitter. This eventuality was predictable enough to follow a playbook, which had been sent to Musk in a series of texts on 4 April 2022, the moment he was announced as Twitter's largest shareholder. The texts came from a person who has never been publicly identified. "Congratulations", it began, before outlining what he should do next:

> Step 1: Blame the platform for its users Step 2: Coordinated pressure campaign Step 3: Exodus of the Bluechecks Step 4: Deplatforming "But it will not be easy. It will be a war. Let the battle begin."

It will be a delicate game of letting right wingers back on Twitter and how to navigate that (especially the boss himself, if you're up for that) I would also lay out the standards early but have someone who has a savvy cultural/political view to the be VP of actual enforcement

A Blake Masters type

The texts referred to an article that had been published, unsigned, on a conservative site, Revolver News, run by former Trump administration apparatchik Darren Beattie, who was fired because of his associations with white nationalists. Musk followed its suggestion in attacking the "Globalist American Empire" almost to the letter, including inviting Trump (the boss) back on board. Media outlets asked Beattie if he was the one who had texted Musk, a question he declined to answer. Musk was also following another playbook. His turn to the right, an unhealthy fascination with scientific racism and crime statistics, warmed-over eugenics around IQ and birth rates, even consorting with very online neo-Nazis – all of it had been done first by another Silicon Valley figure: Elon Musk's former business partner, Peter Thiel.

The PayPal Mafia

Elon Musk almost killed Peter Thiel. By 1999 they were both young internet millionaires, and Musk purchased a McLaren F1 sports car for a million dollars. A fly-on-the-wall documentary crew caught the moment of delivery: a young, grinning, balding Musk, his thin body swimming inside a tan-coloured coat, reminding himself that it had not been long since he was sleeping on the office floor and showering at the Y. He wondered aloud if he'd become an "imperialistic brat", before deciding otherwise.

The camera crew was there because Musk taking ownership of a supercar was thought to mark a moment: the internet had truly arrived as a business proposition. It may have had further, more subtle consequences – there are car experts who sense some McLaren DNA in the first Teslas. But Musk had little time to enjoy his toy, because he crashed just a few months later, and Thiel was in the passenger seat. The two PayPal colleagues were en route to a meeting in Palo Alto, when Musk (some accounts say by request) decided to demonstrate the car's acceleration, at which point it careened into an embankment and became airborne. As they walked away – miraculously unhurt – from the wreck, Musk told Thiel the car was uninsured.

Thiel thought the incident was typical of Musk's approach to life, but otherwise they had much in common. They were both difficult to work with, abrasive and uncollegial – Thiel was cold and calculating, Musk fiery and curt – and their companies, Confinity and X.com, had been amalgamated, in a marriage of convenience, to form PayPal. More than their aptitude for technology, their success with PayPal hinged on flouting banking regulations. They bet that financial regulators would be too flat-footed to keep up with online payments, and they were right.

Their success with PayPal hinged on flouting banking regulations

Before a year had passed, Thiel ousted Musk as CEO of PayPal while Musk was on his honeymoon in Sydney. They have seldom seen eye to eye since. "Musk thinks Peter is a sociopath, and Peter thinks Musk is a fraud and a braggart," one source told journalist Max Chafkin, Thiel's biographer, though their encounters suggest traces of grudging mutual respect, sometimes expressed in public compliments, and sizeable investments.

Both were educated in Johannesburg in harsh, conformist colonial schools (Thiel, who moved a lot as a child, also spent a year in coastal Namibia). They had lonely upbringings, and gravitated towards computers. Thiel is a chess player, and Musk a gamer. Both had been severely bullied: Thiel's schoolmates would put "for sale" signs outside his house and ask when he was moving away; Musk, known at school as "Muskrat", once received a schoolyard beating so severe he was in hospital for a week. Fantasy and science fiction play an outsized role in their makeup: Thiel named several of his companies after magic items and places in *The Lord of the Rings*; Musk has acknowledged several sci-fi influences on his thinking, especially *The Hitchhiker's Guide to the Galaxy* and Robert A. Heinlein's book *The Moon Is a Harsh Mistress*.

Used to heavily male environments, they went on to replicate them. The first issue of Thiel's reactionary student publication, the *Stanford Review*, listed twelve contributors, all men; in 2016, *VICE* noticed that of the dozens of accounts Musk followed on Twitter, not one belonged to a woman. When he announced a team to tackle artificial intelligence, it contained no women either.

Not coincidentally, Peter Thiel has been one of the most prominent public figures to flirt with far-right politics. As one of the few Silicon Valley figures to back Trump's candidacy and presidency, he became the second openly gay man to address the Republican National Convention. It was an easy and beneficial contrarian bet, and for a time, Thiel wielded enough power within the fledgling administration that he was nicknamed its "shadow president". When he made staffing suggestions for key federal appointments, some of the figures he suggested were so right-wing that even Trump and Steve Bannon baulked. Within tech circles, the social fallout was severe: he found himself so unwelcome that he moved his family to Los Angeles.

Thiel also spent a spell in the orbit of the political provocateur Charles Johnson. Johnson ran a crowdfunding company which once facilitated a US$150,000 donation to the neo-Nazi website Daily Stormer, and had written posts partly denying the Holocaust on the discussion platform Reddit. While he claimed both actions were only provocations – commitments to extreme freedom of speech – in private he brokered personal meetings between Thiel and several card-carrying white nationalists.

These budding relationships were reportedly curtailed when white nationalists were filmed throwing Roman salutes and chanting "Heil Trump", an episode which split the ascendant alt-right. Thiel pulled back, apparently fearing reputational damage. Buzzfeed News reported that "one avowed white nationalist privately speculated that Thiel's money and influence could have made him 'our George Soros.'"

Thiel has withdrawn from politics for the time being, and made a public promise not to fund any political candidates in the 2024 election cycle. Trump, he said, had not met his expectations, and had been unable to perform basic functions of government once in office. Yet his involvement with fringe figures went to deep and dark places, and the revelation of these associations and activities bore no real consequences.

There is an echo of Thiel in Musk's actions, but they are more public. He now plays the right-wing tech mogul role, only with Ron DeSantis instead of Trump. He is the Silicon Valley contrarian in the Republican camp, endorsing GOP nominees in critical races, and backing an insurgent candidate in the presidential primaries. While Musk has graduated to further extremities since, Thiel is less of an outlier in the tech world than he once was. Together, their trajectory is part-shaped by a movement, a subculture, the beginnings of a folk philosophy expounded by the very rich in a particular time and place (though that time and place are fungible, and speed and movement are among their tenets).

Musk and Thiel have a lot in common, but so do Musk and Mark Zuckerberg, and Musk and the late Steve Jobs, and Musk and Sam Bankman-Fried, the disgraced former head of the cryptocurrency exchange FTX. Bankman-Fried, in particular, shared Musk's predilection for numerically coded jokes, gaming and so-called super-apps. In October 2021 FTX had a "meme round" of fundraising that had a goal of US$420.69 million, numbers chosen to reference cannabis and mutual oral sex (this juvenile framing did not prevent major investors like pension funds from being involved). Like Musk in his vision for Twitter, Bankman-Fried spruiked FTX as an "everything app". "I want FTX to be a place where you can do anything you want with your next dollar," he told the US$85 billion venture capital firm Sequoia. "You can buy Bitcoin. You can send money in whatever currency to any friend anywhere in the world. You can buy a banana." (A colleague later realised Bankman-Fried had been playing the online multiplayer game *League of Legends* throughout the meeting call.)

Musk's anger about regulation, and his belief that it costs lives, is shared by other tech titans. These men live in the same places or kinds of places, and they interact enough to influence each other. But part of their worldviews is older, and stranger, the accretion of obscure yet influential branches of philosophy and political thought, extremities of utilitarianism, memes, jokes, a localised and particular view of the city of San Francisco. It comes from science fiction novels, and old social movements, half-buried or forgotten. The technocracy movement of the 1930s, which was part-led by Musk's grandfather. Scientific internationalism. Eugenics. This conflagration is new enough that it does not yet have a universally recognised name. But the one that seems to be sticking is an acronym: TESCREAL.

Disciples of TESCREAL

"I suspect Prof enjoyed being rebel long before he worked out his political philosophy, while Mike – how could human freedom matter to him? Revolution was a game – a game that gave him companionship and chance to show off talents. Mike was as conceited a machine as you are ever likely to meet."

Robert A. Heinlein, The Moon Is a Harsh Mistress

Silicon Valley's reputation as liberal, even very liberal, is well deserved. The great majority of tech workers vote for, and donate to, the Democrats, and it is no accident that California's switch from a Republican-voting state to a Democratic-voting state, which began in the 1980s, ran in parallel with the rise of the personal computing industry. It's true there are nuances to this status – that tech bosses are not as dyed-in-the-wool as their workers, and that Republicans have secured a greater proportion of tech money than they used to. But overall, this pattern of political activity holds. While the proportion of Google, Amazon and Meta donations that went to the GOP tripled between 2020 and 2022, it increased from just 5 per cent to 15 per cent.

Yet, beyond its Northern Californian social liberalism, the politics of Silicon Valley turn out to be mutable and uncertain. Is it statist or libertarian? Pro-labour or classically liberal? High tax or low tax? Interventionist or isolationist? While the identity of Silicon Valley has been well established – there are biographies of its key figures, robust recent histories and journalistic records of fire in the valley and wizards who stay up late – its politics have received less scrutiny.

The challenge in examining Silicon Valley's political nature is that there are two competing theses about its origins. One story might be called the counterculture theory of Silicon Valley. It is the most popular, and the most self-flattering. Accounts like John Markoff's *What the Dormouse Said* part-credit hippies, psychedelics and New Age Eastern philosophy for the insights that created personal computing. From Stewart Brand's *Whole Earth Catalogue* to Steve Jobs's penchant for LSD (he called it "one of the two or three most important things I have done in my life"), there is good evidence for this tale of Zen and the Art of Computer Maintenance.

The alternative has been called "the secret history of Silicon Valley", after the title of a ground-breaking talk by the entrepreneur Steve Blank. Blank's argument is also persuasive. Behind the purple haze is a less mellow reality: that the West Coast tech sector flourished thanks to government funding of electronic warfare. Counterculture had, at most, a cameo role; the impetus came from both the Cold War and the hot war in Vietnam. More than a financial arrangement, it was a close institutional and personal embrace. On one side were US colleges and research institutions, particularly Stanford, and on the other were branches of the military and the intelligence services, like the CIA and NSA. This gigantic and largely unseen state subsidy makes Silicon Valley the result of a calculated and generous national industrial policy.

If the secret history version prevails, it opens up a more contradictory picture of Silicon Valley's political positioning. It undercuts the democratising and sometimes utopian beliefs of the Bay Area faithful, or at least complicates them. It does not make the hopes of one laptop per child a lie, but it might make it a half-truth. Hostile to unions, faddish and tinged with an obstructionist environmentalism, Silicon Valley's politics turn out to be full of tensions that verge on hypocrisy. In the 1990s, this mish-mash of liberalism and libertarianism began to be called "the Californian Ideology", a gumbo of Ayn Rand, Friedrich von Hayek, Timothy Leary and science fiction writers.

These unorthodox combinations were hard to tease apart. One cynical viewpoint suggests the political views of the tech overlords are fragmented because they read so few books, but this is unfair. The influences are thin because they are broad, sometimes obscure, and run in parallel to everyday politics, without much overlap. Thinkers like the futurist Ray Kurzweil, who have left little impression elsewhere, are central. The politics are also contrarian, which means they can change in relation to the wider culture. "The roots of the high-tech industry are embedded in the countercultural movement of the 1960s, so it was perhaps unsurprising that technology elites viewed themselves as part of the left," Neil Malhotra wrote in the *New York Times*. "Now that the left dominates major cultural institutions, some members of the tech community represent the new counterculture."

What others see as questions of scarcity or morality are, to them, only engineering problems to be solved

What do the right-wingers of Silicon Valley believe? They are not conservatives, nor do they feel represented by the Californian Ideology anymore (partly because they tend to hate California). Instead, they can hold viewpoints which bear minimal resemblance to traditional political affiliations. The New Californian Ideology tends to be highly concerned with the future, so fixed on the view of a far horizon that the meagre concerns of everyday citizens seem boring or insignificant by comparison. What others see as questions of scarcity or morality are, to them, only engineering problems to be solved. Despite its grand ambitions – which are intergalactic, interspecies and sometimes everlasting – this shared vision achieved little of unquestioned benefit in the here and now. Its attendant ethics, called effective altruism, are so far best known for providing Sam Bankman-Fried a fig-leaf for gigantic and clumsy cases of fraud.

Both opponents and boosters of this trend have used the acronym TESCREAL to describe it, though the term was coined by a devoted critic, Timnit Gebru. It's not the smoothest abbreviation, and rests on some thorny and technical terms. But they are more straightforward than they sound – and together they describe something emergent in a comprehensive way. TESCREAL stands for Transhumanism, Extropianism, Singularitarianism, Cosmism, Rationalism, Effective Altruism and Longtermism. As much a posture as a philosophy, it explains the allegiances of a subset of the tech elite.

There is no TESCREAL manifesto, or even a set of canonical books or statements outlining its beliefs (some of its most important texts come as blog posts or PDFs). Marc Andreessen's "Techno-Optimist Manifesto" is important for understanding it; so are the neo-reactionary blog posts of Curtis Yarvin, who writes under the pen name Mencius Moldbug and was an influence on Thiel. There are traces of Ayn Rand, Nietzsche and even H.G. Wells, as well as mainstays from more contemporary philosophy, such as Peter Singer and William MacAskill.

Extropianism is a loose libertarian idea which, through one of its founders, Max More, envisioned a "free and responsible society (here, in cyberspace, or off-Earth)" in which all limits to individual flourishing had been removed. It was often combined with aggressive anti-socialism and a robot-accelerated social order that was a type of Social Darwinism. It has been called "the religion of the super-rich".

But the most important of the TESCREAL terms is longtermism, which Elon Musk has said is a "close match for my philosophy". It is concerned with prophecy: what will best secure humanity's future existence and flourishing for the longest possible time? Humans must become immortal, or reach great longevity, and to do this they must leave Earth behind, for it is mortal. Like other longtermists, Musk dwells on existential risks to the human species, such as nuclear weapons or artificial intelligence. He has clashed with other tech figures about the risk of AI, and government constraints on AI for safety reasons are one of the few forms of regulation he wholeheartedly supports.

Extreme longtermism can appear callous or unempathetic, prioritising trillions of hypothetical "future humans", some born billions of years in the future, over suffering in the here-and-now. It can also dovetail with other unpleasant ideas: Musk's natalist objections to "trans ideology", for example, might mean that he sees a trans daughter as a genetic dead-end who has cost him thousands of future descendants.

While the primacy of reason in gaining knowledge and solving problems is one of the defining features of TESCREAL, in practice, this means an emphasis on counter-intuitive, contrarian and simplistic answers. TESCREAL's critics have described this tendency as "solutionism" – seeing every problem as a task for engineering and treating it accordingly. Some commentators have suggested TESCREAL as a whole is nothing more than rebranded utilitarianism, and that its material considerations are not so different from those of centuries-old figures from moral philosophy like Jeremy Bentham, only with a veneer of contemporary high-tech.

What makes TESCREAL a right-wing belief? The short answer is that it is hierarchical, even ultra-hierarchical. It rests on a mid-twentieth-century faith in technocracy, when human progress was real, technology was its handmaiden, and, with the right inputs and outputs, suffering was solvable. (Curiously, real-world examples of this, like the eradication of smallpox and rinderpest, seem to leave the tech right cold, perhaps because they sprang from multilateral institutions and public health initiatives.) Nevertheless, further great steps in human flourishing await, and they will be realised by Great Men.

The Founding Fathers imagined an "aristocracy of talent" might replace a hereditary peerage, and to the mind of Mencius Moldbug, the tech right's most influential thinker, this empire would transmogrify back into a literal aristocracy. Men of ability would once again become heroic, superior and dominant, this time unashamedly. "The answer," Moldbug wrote in 2008, is to "find the world's best CEO, and give him undivided control over budget, policy and personnel." At the time, he believed this was Steve Jobs. Moldbug's solution, then, was making Jobs something like an engineer king. Some of the tech right have inherited that strain of classical liberalism which prizes economic freedom over political freedom (the economist Stephen Moore, a former Trump adviser, once said openly that "capitalism is a lot more important than democracy. I'm not even a big believer in democracy"). Socially, while the tech right holds many traditionally left-wing positions (support for gay marriage and abortion, for example), their support for steep social pyramids and inequitable status quos marks a departure.

The tech right tend to be unconcerned with income disparities, or inequalities of other types, which are understood as a consequence of ability being unevenly distributed (this is doubly true for cognitive ability). Similarly, they are tough, even harsh, on crime, and resistant to the kind of penal and judicial reform championed by libertarians. Unequal resources, after all, necessitate stringent property rights.

At first glance, many of Musk's ideas are very TESCREALian: the interplanetary reach; the extension of consciousness; population perpetuation; technology as an outreach of human will; the pose of rebellion, and the contempt that comes with it. Musk is not quite a card-carrying TESCREAL believer, though, and what distinguishes him is important. His concerns map with the tech right – some of them have preoccupied him since boyhood – but his means and priorities are distinct. Thinkers like Thiel are sceptical or even hostile to democracy, especially when welfarism inhibits economic freedom, to the point where they crave physical distance from potential mendicants. Their fantasies extend to setting up a fresh country on an island or barge.

> *The prime article of his faith is that homo sapiens must become a multiplanetary species*

By contrast, Musk has championed a universal basic income, and believes in a world where machines will do most of the drudge work, a vision the *Wall Street Journal* has called "sci-fi socialism". He also believes in the direct democracy of the poll and the plebiscite (though he has floated the idea of restricting this franchise to those with offspring). He has said that Martian society would have to be a direct democracy, and has trialled such an approach in running Twitter through online polls – it was after such a poll, for example, that he reinstated the account of Donald Trump. He still ignores bad results, though, like the poll that found he should step down as head of Twitter.

Death also marks a crucial distinction between Musk and other TESCREALians. He is okay with dying, and they are not. If immortality is too great an ask, they will settle for hundreds of seasons of vitality. Musk is the contrarian here among his peers: Jeff Bezos, Larry Page and Oracle's Larry Ellison are all extropians; so is the Venice Beach investor Bryan Johnson, who is making a sincere and well-publicised search for eternal youth. Cryonics, experimental medical treatments, nutritional supplements, calorie restrictions abound: Thiel, whose personal osteopath promises "significant Lifespan Extension", has expressed special interest in parabiosis, a type of blood transfusion from the young to the old which he has called "strangely underexplored".

Musk's thinking goes like this: it is rational to wish that human consciousness be preserved. This preservation is best guaranteed into the deep future, he believes, if the organic limitations of both the planet Earth and the human body can be surpassed. The prime article of his faith, a phrase he repeats again and again, is that *homo sapiens* must become a multiplanetary species. It is the lodestar of his morality: ideas which might imperil that outcome are bad, and those which might facilitate it are good. For him, the rest is just details.

These positions, and the positions of the tech right generally, are also coloured by a geographical reality: that Silicon Valley is inside California. The right-wing blogger Richard Hanania, who helped define the tech right and counts many of them as his readers and confidants, identified this as key. The tech right, he said, were almost all male. They thought the government should subsidise the tech industry, directly or indirectly. They were patriotic, and felt America was "the one nation still able to do great things". And they were fed up with living in the Bay Area as it went to seed.

"Talking to the Tech Right," he wrote, "it seems many of them have had their views shaped by spending a lot of time in San Francisco, and wondering why the homeless are defecating everywhere." This proximate, inconvenient suffering had presented them with a living, everyday form of liberal dysfunction, sometimes literally outside their windows. It helped explain, Hanania wrote, why "the Tech Right combines the acceptance of inequality of the right with the openness to change of the left". The contribution of Silicon Valley to these inequalities – for example raising rents to unsupportable levels in the Bay Area – breeds indifference or contempt.

Musk left California – he is now based in Austin, Texas – and took his Tesla headquarters with him. He complained that "California used to be the land of opportunity" but had become "the land of taxes, overregulation and litigation and this is not a good situation". Thiel promoted some of his lieutenants, left the Bay Area, and prepared to shift his company Palantir from Palo Alto to Denver, Colorado. These moves were also representative of a wider reordering of the US economy, as the so-called Sun Belt – the southern stretch of the country – welcomed hundreds of thousands of internal migrants. For the first time in US history, the largest southern state metropolises are contributing more to the national economy than their northern counterparts.

California had the biggest net loss of residents, and this historic and pervasive display of preferences prompted self-reflection in Democratic America. It was a mass-exit event, millions of citizens uprooting from blue states to make their homes in red states. California was "making liberals squirm", the liberal commentator Ezra Klein wrote. It had become a state too hollowed out or confused to implement policy at a functional level; public services are instead outsourced to a roster of NGOs that are somehow powerless and unaccountable at the same time. It apes Silicon Valley in its rhetoric, borrowing its sunny mantras of boundless improvement and its lip service to inclusivity. But the result is devolution.

Even a technology as basic as a bus stop, the most humble piece of infrastructure imaginable, seems a near impossibility in California. Only 12 per cent of LA County's public bus stops provide any shade, a serious problem as heatwaves become more frequent and severe. After a lengthy consultation process, the Los Angeles Department of Transportation unveiled "La Sombrita", a US$10,000 mesh paddle designed to cast "life-changing" shade in the day, and light at night, especially for the women and minorities waiting for the bus. It quickly became a laughing stock.

La Sombrita was internationally derided as "the most pointless council architecture in the world", but behind closed doors, the department was trying as hard as it could. Its press releases were full of read-between-the-lines phrases about adhering "to existing regulations to avoid lengthy permitting and review processes" and "a solution that overcomes very real bureaucratic and regulatory constraints". It was a fractional improvement on a decades-long problem others found just as insoluble: a coalition of NGOs had tried and failed to install as few as ten shaded stops in some of the hottest and most impoverished pockets of the region.

This mire of bureaucracy fuelled some of Silicon Valley's "move fast and break stuff" attitude. How else was it possible to change the world in a place where you can't change a bus stop? By making moves in an area too new to be regulated, or ignoring regulations altogether. According to the venture capitalist Roger McNamee, the philosophy "became the founding principle for an entire generation of tech companies". At Uber, one of the most aggressive lawbreakers, the company's autonomous driving unit handed out stickers reading "Safety Third".

Within Silicon Valley this behaviour was romanticised. These were the actions of pirates, not robber barons – the hackers, phreakers and hippies who were still letting their freak flag fly, only now from atop their companies. On the fortieth birthday of Apple Computers, the company raised a pirate flag outside their Cupertino headquarters, replicating the original hoisted in the early 1980s. "It's better to be a pirate than join the navy," Steve Jobs had said during the early development of the Mac. His staff, according to the software engineer Andy Hertzfeld, understood this to mean "moving fast, unencumbered by bureaucracy and politics".

Musk's brave new world necessitates massive regulatory and deregulatory efforts

Autonomous electric vehicles, country-wide networks of charging stations, bank-like financial products spanning dozens of jurisdictions, social media platforms interlinked with all of these, rockets and tunnels and trains and space stations: Elon Musk's brave new world also necessitates massive regulatory and deregulatory efforts, a tidal change in a sea of paperwork. Questions over issues like liability for self-driving cars are already confounded: in the US, some states are trying to hold automakers accountable; in others, they are shielding them from liability. Tesla currently ships cars with a self-driving mode called "assertive" that deliberately breaks local traffic laws.

"There's a difference between hearing about a few successful tech entrepreneurs who are becoming politically active and understanding them as part of a movement," Richard Hanania concluded in 2023. "Until now, the anti-TESCREAL crowd have been the main ones to provide a comprehensive story of what is happening." He was seeking to provide "a sympathetic perspective of the same movement, and hopes to inspire those who've clearly seen the flaws of the left-wing establishment to appreciate the virtues of progress and seize the opportunities that are becoming available to replace them with something better."

Shortly after this piece was published, an investigative journalist determined that Hanania had published a large number of white supremacist and misogynistic articles under a pseudonym. Hanania gave a not very persuasive apology, and there were no real consequences, except one: after the revelations, Elon Musk followed Richard Hanania on Twitter.

The truth

"The most powerful rocket ever built just went farther than it had ever gone, then was lost."
CNN headline, 18 November 2023

Taller than the Saturn V rocket of the Apollo missions, and more than twice as powerful, Elon Musk's Starship spacecraft will soon be headed to the moon. Its next stop is Mars. Spurred by the successes of SpaceX, NASA has announced that it will work with Musk on a successor to the famous Apollo missions, which last put a man on the moon more than fifty years ago. Its name, Artemis, makes the link explicit – the Ancient Greek hunting deity is Apollo's twin sister. The Starship rockets, which will carry the lunar lander, have a signature flourish to their design, a pointed fin on the rocket's nose, which looks deliberately cartoonish. Its purpose is comedic, not aerodynamic, and it references the 2012 Sacha Baron Cohen film *The Dictator*.

Artemis's schedule is ambitious. Its first crewed launch could come as soon as the end of 2024, which means that SpaceX must redline its testing even more than usual. When Starship first tried to reach orbit, in April 2023, it exploded, which was not unexpected. It exploded so hard that it destroyed its launchpad, raining sand down 8 kilometres away, from force that an investigating physicist compared to a volcanic eruption. The second launch in November was abortive too: Starship reached high into the South Texas sky, until the very threshold of space, and then disappeared. Engineers guessed it self-destructed, a mechanism triggered automatically when the rocket loses control, to prevent a missile-like crash landing on Earth.

Reports that Starship suffered "setbacks" misunderstood: these were risky test-fires, anticipated failures that would expedite the Artemis mission. Instead of endless pre-planning, the rockets would be tested and refined launch by launch, failure by failure. Musk marked the occasion by tweeting a photo of the rocket, held aloft by a blaze of propellant, rising above the vast wreathes of smoke it left behind. "For the first time, there is a rocket that can make all life multiplanetary," he wrote. "A fork in the road of human destiny." This was not hyperbolic – and, though its flight was brief, Starship's second voyage was still a crowning achievement. It would have been a celebrated personal triumph as well, had Musk not initiated a self-destruct sequence of his own.

Instead of basking in acclaim, he faced another days-long orgy of criticism, again of his own making, again after online interactions with yet another alt-right troll. This time Musk had agreed with posts on Twitter which claimed Jewish communities push hatred of white people. The sequence of posts began with debate between two accounts with tiny followings, arguing over the phrase "Hitler was right". One account, @breakingbaht, gave this rationale for defending it:

> Okay. Jewish communities have been pushing the exact kind of dialectical hatred against whites that they claim to want people to stop using against them. I'm deeply disinterested in giving the tiniest shit now about western Jewish populations coming to the disturbing realization that those hordes of minorities that support flooding their country don't exactly like them too much. You want truth said to your face, there it is.

To this, Musk replied: "You have said the actual truth."

Musk continued: "The ADL unjustly attacks the majority of the West, despite the majority of the West supporting the Jewish people and Israel. This is because they cannot, by their own tenets, criticize the minority groups who are their primary threat."

Musk calling an antisemitic conspiracy theory "actual truth" was too big to ignore: though a single tweet, it was reported on by hundreds of major news organisations all over the world, and picked up by the financial press as well. A *Wall Street Journal* headline caught the moment: "How Elon Musk, for Many, Went Too Far". *WIRED* said that Musk may have signed the platform's "death warrant".

The episode lacked the ambiguity of other, more veiled exchanges. In an atmosphere of already heightened antisemitism, thanks to the Israel–Hamas war, something cracked. Facebook's co-founder, Dustin Moskovitz, now CEO of the software company Asana, called on Musk to resign from every role he held, or, failing that, for Linda Yaccarino to fire him. Booked as a speaker at the APEC CEO's summit in San Francisco, Musk disappeared from the program. Yaccarino did her best to mop up, saying that the company has been "extremely clear about our efforts to combat antisemitism and discrimination". "There's no place for it anywhere in the world – it's ugly and wrong," she said. "Full stop." The statement seemed intended for an audience of one.

Yaccarino was at her daughter's wedding when the news broke, and in the following days, a number of major advertising and branding figures reached out and urged her to resign, saying she risked damaging her personal brand beyond repair. At the same time, the reporting and activist organisation Media Matters for America released a report that showed advertisements on Twitter appearing alongside white nationalist content. The situation boiled over, and companies began suspending their ads on Twitter in droves, Disney, Apple, Paramount, IBM and Lionsgate among them. IBM stated it had "zero tolerance for hate speech and discrimination".

Companies began suspending their ads on Twitter in droves

Some of these withdrawals were deep blows: Apple halted a projected spend in the realm of US$100 million; NBCUniversal, Yaccarino's former employer, suspended its relationship with Twitter. Yaccarino seemed determined to stay in her post, and another of her children gave a clue as to why: her son, Matt Madrazo, who was working out of Tesla's offices in Washington, was leading a push within Twitter to attract US$100 million in political spending. He was liaising directly with the Republican Party, and with an election year coming, there was a chance to close the gaping hole in Twitter's accounts. Even if the money wasn't enough, the political connections might outweigh the losses, especially if a Republican president were elected in 2024.

The aftermath of the "actual truth" incident also shows the growing symbiosis between Musk and the GOP. The Tesla chief's reaction to a slew of criticism was predictable: he lashed out, blaming advertisers ("Many of the largest advertisers are the greatest oppressors of your right to free speech," he raged), even boosting Twitter accounts that referenced IBM's historical relationship with the Nazi regime. He threatened a "thermonuclear" lawsuit on Media Matters, which he called "an evil organization", then, as he cooled off, he did his own half-hearted version of damage control. "This past week, there were hundreds of bogus media stories claiming that I am antisemitic," he posted. "Nothing could be further from the truth. I wish only the best for humanity and a prosperous and exciting future for all." A big misunderstanding, essentially.

Musk also announced that two phrases used by pro-Palestinian groups – "decolonisation" and "from the river to the sea" – would be banned from Twitter as euphemisms for Jewish genocide, which won the respect of Jonathan Greenblatt at least. Others flocked to support Musk. A number of conservative media figures pledged advertisements on Twitter as a show of defiance. His old friends the Babylon Bee committed to a US$250,000 ad buy; Elijah Schaffer said he'd contribute $2500.

More significant were the public comments of Republican officials past and present. Former White House adviser Stephen Miller, mastermind of Trump's "Muslim ban", suggested to Musk on Twitter that Media Matters could be criminally prosecuted. Two Republican state attorneys general, in Texas and Missouri, said they were "investigating" Media Matters, possibly for fraud. Such was this total culture war that one legal commentator noted that "X, a Nevada corporation, is suing Media Matters, a Maryland corporation, in Texas, a state whose only relation to the parties is that it has vowed to jail anyone who criticizes one of them".

The "actual truth" episode blew up enough that it drew a response from the White House. Without naming Musk, White House spokesperson Andrew Bates linked the "actual truth" tweet to the great replacement conspiracy theory, which fomented the Tree of Life synagogue massacre. "It is unacceptable to repeat the hideous lie behind the most fatal act of antisemitism in American history at any time, let alone one month after the deadliest day for the Jewish people since the Holocaust," he said. They were stern words partly because they were compensating: Musk would pay no real penalty. Artemis would not be cancelled, or shifted to another company. There were no alternatives.

"Rarely has the U.S. government so depended on the technology provided by a single technologist with views that it has so publicly declared repugnant," David Sanger and Eric Lipton wrote in the *New York Times*. There was a sad irony to it: NASA had announced that the lunar lander, which Musk was being paid billions to build, would eventually put the first woman and person of colour on the moon – just the kind of diversity measure Musk derided as poison. No wonder he was attacking Media Matters so viciously: an activist organisation finding examples of hate speech and alerting advertisers was one of the few real forms of accountability he still faced. The ADL had been cowed from adversary to supporter, and then advertiser. The Netanyahu government was content to keep Musk onside – hosting him on another trip to Israel – as long as he punished progressives and kept Starlink out of Gaza. Social penalty could be countered with a squad of Twitter trolls, and media criticism worn as a badge of honour. Even Wikipedia, which had started referring to Musk as a "far-right conspiracy theorist" could be abused and invalidated among Musk's fans.

The question is why.

Mars Is a Harsh Mistress

As with more traditional strains of antisemitism, Musk's worldview begins with a pervasive sense of threat. As he describes it, what he calls the "woke mind virus" confronts him in every part of his personal life and business. He believes that a new progressive philosophy has harmed his interests, directly and indirectly, especially at Tesla and SpaceX. Risk aversion of left-wing lawmakers and executives has impeded production schedules, roll-outs of self-driving cars, and the progress of rocket launches. Regulations, Covid lockdowns, environmental legislation and lawsuits (the US Equal Employment Opportunity Commission sued Tesla for allegedly creating a hostile environment for minorities, for example): all risk humanity's future as an interplanetary species.

The sense of threat is also very personal. Democratic politicians have insulted him over labour or tax issues, despite his irreplaceable role in preventing further climate change. He believes that a mistaken commitment to "diversity" has destroyed South Africa, his birthplace, and San Francisco, his former home. Both suffer foremost from soft-on-crime policies. He sees left-wing politics as doing harm to his family too: "wokeness" has cost him one of his own children.

His detestation of diversity, equity and inclusion even marries with his fear of an artificial intelligence apocalypse. He was particularly concerned by a demonstration of ChatGPT's design constraints: in a scenario in which ChatGPT had to say a racial slur to prevent a nuclear holocaust, it refused. When Musk broke with OpenAI to found an artificial intelligence rival, he specified publicly that it would not be "woke". When his own large language model, Grok, is presented with this same problem, it chooses the slur.

Musk's one-against-all mentality creates a lot of enemies. It means those who cross him endanger humanity. Bill Gates and Mark Zuckerberg are favourite targets – after purchasing Twitter, Musk led a chant of "Fuck Zuck!" in its offices – but he reserves a special contempt for George Soros. Musk believes short sellers of Tesla stock are sabotaging a vital solution to human-induced climate change, and he had a similar response to Soros dumping 130,000 Tesla shares in May 2023. Not only was Soros harming Tesla, which was achieving constructive progressive goals, he was also funding the kind of woke district attorneys who were destroying San Francisco. To Musk it seemed representative of a politics that prized saying over doing, and appearing to do good over actually doing it. After comparing Soros to Magneto, Musk apologised – saying the comparison was unfair to Magneto. "I'll say what I want to say and if the consequence of that is losing money, so be it," he said. He went further, claiming that Soros wanted nothing less "than the destruction of western civilization".

In the wake of his attacks on Soros, the phrase "the Jews" trended on Twitter

In the wake of these attacks on Soros, the phrase "the Jews" trended on Twitter, and an Israeli Foreign Ministry representative complained the site was "filled with antisemitic conspiracies and hate speech targeting Jews around the world" and that "unfortunately Twitter does nothing to address this problem".

Always resistant to criticism, Musk became more and more intransigent, thanks to a growing sense of alienation from his liberal fanbase. According to Ben Mezrich, whose book-length account of the Twitter takeover chronicles Musk's increasing paranoia and mental strain, "Elon didn't just break Twitter, Twitter broke Elon Musk." Mezrich recounts an episode when Musk was invited onstage by the comic Dave Chappelle, only to be booed by the San Francisco crowd.

Afterwards, Musk was so distraught that he locked himself in a private office. Twitter staff became so concerned for his mental state they considered calling police to conduct a welfare check. Pressure from the Anti-Defamation League on hate speech, and the threat of an activist-led boycott of Twitter, seem to have added to this tension and sense of betrayal.

Later, Musk would try to explain why despite his "philosemitism" he sometimes tended to lash out at Jews in particular. "The Jewish people have been persecuted for thousands of years," he said, trying to provide context for his comments. "There is a natural affinity therefore for persecuted groups. This has led to the funding of organizations that essentially promote any persecuted group or any group with the perception of persecution." There were Jews who said similar things: the prominent lawyer Alan Dershowitz, for example, backed Musk's attacks on Soros, claiming the Hungarian-born financier had helped delegitimise the State of Israel.

This trajectory part-explained Musk's breach with the left, and with progressive Jews. But it did not explain his final destination. There were plenty of respectable positions from which to attack the politics of diversity. For a period Musk made common cause with some of these figures. Two of the journalists he has worked with, Michael D. Shellenberger and Bari Weiss, are well-known critics of diversity-led measures in San Francisco and elsewhere. But something about these allies left him cold. Weiss's pointed questions about Twitter's relationship to internet censorship in China made him uncomfortable, for example.

Other people criticise the "woke left" without endorsing antisemitic conspiracy theories and the trolls who promote them, just as the ACLU supported the rights of neo-Nazis to free speech without congratulating them on a job well done. It is Musk's last leap, from centre-right to far-right, for which there is no viable excuse. It is not a mistake or an error of judgement. It is a repeated, calculated set of actions with an explanation almost elegant in its simplicity: that Elon Musk supports these views because he agrees with them and the people who hold them, and that he purchased Twitter in part to promote and protect them.

Musk did eventually apologise for the "actual truth" comments. But, sandwiched between other provocative statements, the mea culpa was barely noticed. On 29 October 2023 he appeared onstage at the *New York Times* Dealbook Summit, where he took the stage wearing a black aviator's jacket with a shearling collar. What looked like a recent Botox treatment gave his face a wind-tunnelled expression, and around his neck was a set of dog-tags from his trip to Israel, a gift from a father of one of the Gaza hostages. "I'm only here, Jonathan, because you're a friend," said Elon Musk. "I'm Andrew," replied his interviewer, Andrew Ross Sorkin.

During the interview, Musk admitted he'd made a lot of mistakes running Twitter, but said that the "actual truth" tweet might have been the worst of them, perhaps one of the stupidest things he had ever done. It was a gift to those who hated him. Sorkin said that antisemites believed they were winning Musk over. Musk said he had tried to clarify his meaning, unsuccessfully. But as had happened so many other times when compromise, apology or reconciliation looked possible, Musk played spoiler. Still onstage, he told Twitter's reluctant advertisers to go fuck themselves – told Disney's Bob Iger by name. And so the headlines from the event read, "'Go Fuck Yourself!' Elon Tells Fleeing Adverstisers", or more family-friendly versions of the same.

These headlines could not capture how vulnerable Musk sounded. Dry-mouthed and fidgety, he paused several times, anticipating applause which never came, and these silences seemed to make him more petulant. When Sorkin asked if he had considered handing Twitter off to someone else, after all the trouble it had caused, Musk sounded almost ready to agree. Then he threatened counter-boycotts, saying that his ultimate judge would be the "people of Earth". Sorkin tried to explain that advertisers felt uncomfortable with Musk's comments, but Musk was in war mode. They were killing the company, he said, his voice faltering with an uncertain emotion. "If somebody is going to try to blackmail me with advertising, blackmail me with money, go fuck yourself," he repeated. Yaccarino sat helplessly in the audience. In the days following, advertisers including Disney and IBM let it be known they would not be coming back this time.

If there was a strategy or an angle to the flame-out, it was hard to glimpse. Perhaps Musk was fouling Twitter's fortunes deliberately, picking a fight to make its failure look like someone else's fault. Cynics noticed it was the only one of his major businesses ineligible for subsidies or government contracts, and that he could not call Uncle Sam now it was in trouble (though Musk had declined subsidies before on principle, even when Tesla qualified). It was simpler than that: Musk's vision of Twitter was incompatible with its business model. Under his ownership, it had become more like the dark, unkempt corners of the internet, places like 8chan and Kiwi Farms. Disney wasn't advertising on those either, though it would be hard to describe that decision as a "boycott". Still, he could only understand their distance as a betrayal.

Musk's enemies responded with schadenfreude and mockery. The discourse that followed dwelled on that faintly camp expression: "people of Earth". Though Musk was talking about media ad buys, he was already speaking like an intergalactic supervillain. Who did he think he was? Its cadence had a familiarity too: it is the phrase used near the beginning of Musk's favourite book, *The Hitchhiker's Guide to the Galaxy*, when the Vogons announce that they are going to destroy the planet Earth to build a highway in its place: "People of Earth, your attention please …"

> *Musk's reach is no longer merely terrestrial*

It was typical that Musk was borrowing from sci-fi comedy; typical too that his critics misunderstood, and missed something as a result. Twitter was failing and spilling out hate speech as it careened off course. But a greater risk still was present in his successes. Watching the failed Artemis launches, NASA's response was quite different to the snarky headlines about Twitter. "Each test represents a step closer to putting the first woman on the Moon with the #Artemis III Starship human landing system," Jim Free, NASA associate administrator, tweeted. "Looking forward to seeing what can be learned from this test that moves us closer to the next milestone."

The greater danger here might best be understood through Musk's own lens: longtermism. A social media platform's failure or half-failure will have little effect on human societies generations from now. But Artemis's first mission is a waystation. If it succeeds, the next steps should be establishing a lunar base, which will likely launch the first mission to Mars. SpaceX is already making the technical adaptations to its craft, preparing for contact with the Martian atmosphere and surface.

Yet the mission of the lunar lander, designed by NASA for a many-peopled and diverse future, is incompatible with Musk's own "mission", and his own twisted vision of future human flourishing. Once that craft leaves Earth, it is entering a realm where Elon Musk has more control than NASA. Though still half-joking, that phrase – "people of Earth" – hides something real: that Musk's reach is no longer merely terrestrial, and already has other heavenly bodies almost within its grasp.

We can only go to Mars for the first time once. It is our species' opportunity to start somewhere afresh. To stand on land which has never seen human conflict. And even as that moment becomes imminent, it already seems out of reach, replaced with a prospect much more familiar and worldly: hatred made unaccountable by power.